Oxford School *Shakespeare*

AS YOU LIKE IT

edited by
Roma Gill, OBE
M.A. *Cantab.*, B. Litt. *Oxon*

OXFORD
UNIVERSITY PRESS

OXFORD
UNIVERSITY PRESS

Great Clarendon Street, Oxford OX2 6DP

Oxford University Press is a department of the University of Oxford.
It furthers the University's objective of excellence in research,
scholarship, and education by publishing worldwide in

Oxford   New York

Auckland   Cape Town   Dar es Salaam   Hong Kong   Karachi
Kuala Lumpur   Madrid   Melbourne   Mexico City   Nairobi
New Delhi   Shanghai   Taipei   Toronto

With offices in

Argentina   Austria   Brazil   Chile   Czech Republic   France   Greece
Guatemala   Hungary   Italy   Japan   Poland   Portugal   Singapore
South Korea   Switzerland   Thailand   Turkey   Ukraine   Vietnam

Oxford is a registered trade mark of Oxford University Press
in the UK and in certain other countries

© Oxford University Press 1977

Reprinted in this new edition 2009

The moral rights of the author have been asserted

Database right Oxford University Press (maker)

British Library Cataloguing in Publication Data

Data available

ISBN 978-0-19-832869-8

20 19 18 17 16 15 14 13 12

Printed in Great Britain by CPI Group (UK) Ltd., Croydon CR0 4YY

The Publisher would like to thank the
following for permission to reproduce
photographs:

pp. xxviii, 8, 16, 24, 32, 42, 46, 60, 90, 103
Donald Cooper/Photostage; p. 126 Richard
Kalina

Cover Artwork by Silke Bachmann
Illustrations by Alexy Pendle

Oxford School Shakespeare
edited by Roma Gill
with additional material by Judith Kneen

Macbeth
Much Ado About Nothing
Henry V
Romeo and Juliet
A Midsummer Night's Dream
Twelfth Night
Hamlet
The Merchant of Venice
Othello
Julius Caesar
The Tempest
The Taming of the Shrew
King Lear
As You Like It
Antony and Cleopatra
Measure for Measure
Henry IV Part I
The Winter's Tale
Coriolanus
Love's Labour's Lost
Richard II

Contents

Introduction

About the Play

As You Like It! The title promises everything—and gives away nothing: the master craftsman of the Elizabethan theatre knew how to keep his audiences guessing—and knew exactly how they like their comedies, whether at the end of the sixteenth century or the beginning of the twenty-first. Romance without sentimentality but with a hint of danger; satire without cruelty; topical relevance which will not be too controversial; and something to think about on the way home that won't lead to argument and civil disturbance. Add a song or two perhaps—and certainly a good measure of double entendres (which can be enjoyed or ignored as you please).

And the main theme? Women in Love.

This seems to have been Shakespeare's personal recipe for success, explored and perfected through eight early comedies which all centre on the love affairs of two young women and their chosen partners—men who are usually far less dynamic, less individualized, than these spirited and resourceful girls. Their parts are some of the most attractive roles for women in all English drama. But in Shakespeare's theatre there were no female actors, and not for another hundred years would it be socially acceptable for women to perform on public stages in England. The female parts were originally played by young boys, their voices not yet broken, who were apprenticed to older actors in the dramatic company, the Lord Chamberlain's Men, for which Shakespeare was what we would now call the 'resident dramatist'.

This convention of boy-plays-girl was of course accepted without question by all who wrote for the Elizabethan theatre, but Shakespeare took a particular delight in *doubling* this cross-dressing—so that his boys-as-girls quickly become girls-as-boys, offering endless opportunities for joking, dramatic irony, and sexual double entendres.

In *As You Like It* Rosalind (who has suddenly fallen head-over-heels in love with Orlando) is driven from her cruel uncle's court to take refuge in the Forest of Arden, disguising herself as a boy to protect herself and her cousin Celia. But the doublet and hose of her gender-swapping must conceal her emotions as well as her person in her next encounter with Orlando—who has also escaped into the Forest to avoid his brother's murderous intentions.

The plot is pretty, not profound; and the outcome is predictable from the beginning. The Forest may be a lonely, 'desert' place, but it is here that lovers are united, enmities reconciled, and the true values of civilization are restored.

The play might well have been intended as some kind of showpiece for the opening of the new Globe Theatre in 1599, demonstrating the many talents of the Chamberlain's Men as well as the magnificence of their playhouse. A new comedian, Robert Armin, had just joined the company, bringing a sophisticated wit well suited to the role of Jaques—and that character's famous oration ('All the world's a stage ...' 2, 7, 139–66) could easily be an eloquent gesture in the direction of the motto now waving proudly above the heads of audience and actors alike: *Totus mundus agit histrionem* (all the world plays the actor).

Leading Characters in the Play

Duke Senior The rightful duke, who has been deposed by his younger brother and now lives in exile in the Forest of Arden with a number of lords who have also been deprived of their estates.

Duke Frederick The younger brother of Duke Senior, who now rules over his court and is feared rather than loved by those who serve him.

Rosalind The daughter of Duke Senior who has remained at court as a companion for Celia. When Duke Frederick suddenly becomes suspicious of her, she disguises herself as a boy (calling herself 'Ganymede') and goes to find her father in the Forest.

Celia Duke Frederick's daughter, who accompanies her banished cousin into the Forest disguised as a country girl called 'Aliena'.

Oliver The eldest son of Sir Roland de Boys, who has inherited the greatest part of his father's property. Without any reason but jealousy, he is plotting to kill his younger brother

Orlando who has all the excellent qualities of a gentleman, despite the fact that Oliver has prevented him from being properly educated.

Touchstone A professional jester who accompanies Rosalind and Celia into the Forest.

Jaques A melancholy traveller who has followed Duke Senior into the Forest and entertains the lords with his criticism of society.

Adam An old servant of Sir Roland de Boys. He represents the honesty and loyalty which the modern world (represented by Oliver de Boys) does not value.

Corin A wise old shepherd; although he is simple, he is by no means foolish.

Silvius   A silly young shepherd, whose only desire in life is to win the love of Phoebe.

Phoebe   A young shepherdess. She is cruel to Silvius and mocks his poems, until she falls passionately in love with 'Ganymede' (who of course is Rosalind in disguise).

Synopsis

As You Like It: commentary

Scene 1   Orlando opens the play with a long speech addressed to Adam. It is a
clumsy way of giving information to an audience, but the information
is essential, not only for understanding the plot. Orlando introduces
one of the play's important themes, the nature of a gentleman. As the
son of Sir Roland de Boys, Orlando is a gentleman by birth, but he has
been deprived of a gentleman's education by his brother. When
Orlando and Oliver confront each other, there is no doubt about which
is the true heir to Sir Roland. Oliver possesses his father's lands, but
there is no trace of Sir Roland's honourable nature in his character.
When he slanders Orlando to Charles, the duke's wrestler, and urges
Charles to kill him in the wrestling match, Oliver shows how malicious
and unnatural he is. At the end of the scene he admits that he has no
cause to hate his brother, and then reveals his motive for wanting
Orlando to be killed: Orlando has many virtues, and is very popular,

> and indeed so much in the heart of the world, and especially of
> my own people, who best know him, that I am altogether
> misprized.   (1, 1, 151–3)

Shakespeare is very interested in jealousy arising out of such a situation;
he studies it again in this play, and in a later play, *King Lear*, he shows
how it can bring about a tragic catastrophe.

   Another theme is introduced in this scene when Charles tells Oliver
that the outlawed Duke Senior and his loyal supporters have gone into
the Forest of Arden,

> and fleet the time carelessly as they did in the golden world.
>   (1, 1, 108–9)

The Golden Age (or 'world') was created by Greek and Latin poets.
They claimed that it existed many thousands of years ago, before men
lived in cities and were cruel. It was a pastoral existence: people lived in
the country, and found their food growing around them. There was no
need to work for a living; no animals were slaughtered for meat; people
spent their time singing, dancing, and writing poetry. Many English
writers at the time of Shakespeare found the pastoral conventions very
attractive. Some poets, such as Sir Philip Sidney, wrote of shepherds

whose entire existence was given to worshipping the shepherdesses whom they loved: in the play, Silvius is typical of such shepherd-poets. Other poets, like Edmund Spenser, made their shepherds speak social criticism, often comparing court or city life, full of envy and ambition, with the peace and contentment of country life: Duke Senior, in *Act 2, Scene 1*, utters such conventional remarks.

The first scene of the play, then, starts off one of the two central actions of the complex plot. It also introduces three themes: the nature of a gentleman; the envy that is provoked by goodness; and the 'golden world' of pastoral convention. Each of these topics will be examined again—perhaps more than once—in the course of the play.

Scene 2   The second scene introduces new characters and begins the second main action of the play. When we first see Rosalind, in this scene, she is unhappy, and we are never allowed to forget this for very long. Rosalind is usually gay and witty, not because she is light-hearted and carefree, but because she has courage and can hide her sorrows. She decides that she will play at falling in love, and Celia warns her not to be too serious about this. Later in the play, we remember this warning.

Rosalind and Celia are both fond of making puns; many writers at the time of Shakespeare enjoyed this playing with words. In the English language, a lot of words have more than one meaning and some words, which have different meanings and different spellings, sound alike (for instance 'pear', 'pair', and 'pare'). A pun is made when someone amuses himself by reacting to one meaning of a word when the speaker had intended another: for instance

> **Touchstone**
> Nay, if I keep not my rank—
> **Rosalind**
> Thou loosest thy old smell.   (1, 2, 95–6)

The word 'rank' can mean both 'position' (which Touchstone intends), and 'stench' (which Rosalind pretends to understand).

Touchstone takes no part in the action of the play, but he is very valuable for his observations, full of common-sense, on the ridiculous aspects of the other characters. When Le Beau tells Rosalind and Celia that they have 'lost much good sport' (1, 2, 89) because they have not seen a wrestling match in which a young man broke three ribs, Touchstone pretends to be glad that he has learned something new:

> Thus men may grow wiser every day. It is the first time that ever
> I heard breaking of ribs was sport for ladies.   (*1*, *2*, 121–2)

Touchstone is not stupid; he is a professional comedian. For hundreds
of years before the time of Shakespeare, the kings of England employed
such jesters as court fools, whose duties were to entertain the monarch
at mealtimes, and at any other time when the king wished to be amused.
Fools were permitted to speak freely, and to comment on current affairs
and prominent personalities. They were the first English satirists. The
fool's position had its dangers; if the fool gave offence, he was likely to
be whipped (see *1*, *2*, *76*). The fool usually wore a distinctive 'motley'
costume of green and yellow but Touchstone seems to abandon this
professional dress while he is in the Forest. Celia's description of
Touchstone as 'our whetstone' (*1*, *2*, *50*) points to another of the fool's
functions. By appearing stupid, the fool gave other men a chance to
make fun of him and show how witty they could be. He was what we
now call a 'stooge'.

When Le Beau comes on to the stage, Celia greets him in French.
This was the language used in the English court after the Norman
conquest of England in 1066. Some people thought that to be able to
speak French was a sign of good education, but there were other people,
especially at the time of Shakespeare, who thought it was a ridiculous
affectation. Celia makes fun of Le Beau and his formal speech. By
calling the wrestling 'sport', and suggesting that the ladies would have
liked to see the deaths of three fine young men, Le Beau shows the
inhumanity of court life. His callousness contrasts with the tenderness
and care that Rosalind and Celia show when they try to dissuade
Orlando from fighting.

Rosalind's remarks to Orlando, and about him, reveal how quickly
she is falling in love. At the end of the scene Orlando too admits to
himself that he is overcome with a new emotion. Both Rosalind and
Orlando have demonstrated an ability to use words well and wittily, but
at this moment neither of them is able to express these new feelings.
Rosalind can only tell Orlando, obliquely,

> you have wrestled well and overthrown
> More than your enemies.   (*1*, *2*, 228–9)

Orlando cannot speak at all until Rosalind has left the stage, and then
he is amazed to find himself so tongue-tied:

> What passion hangs these weights upon my tongue?
> I cannot speak to her, yet she urg'd conference.   (*1*, *2*, 231–2)

After the wrestling match, we should have a good opinion of Orlando's strength. He showed moral courage when he defied his brother, and again when he politely refused to change his mind about fighting Charles. The fight has proved his physical strength—and after this the character can afford to indulge his romantic passion in the Forest.

When Le Beau returns to warn Orlando that he must leave the court, he is not the same as the affected courtier that he appeared to be when he first came on to the stage. What he says about Duke Frederick shows that he is aware of danger in the court, and knows he must be cautious about speaking his mind:

> The duke is humorous: what he is indeed
> More suits you to conceive than I to speak of.　　(1, 2, 240–1)

He prepares us for the duke's anger with Rosalind, and renews one of the play's main themes when he tells us that the anger is

> Grounded upon no other argument
> But that the people praise her for her virtues.　　(1, 2, 253–4)

Scene 3　Although Celia and Rosalind are laughing about Rosalind's love for Orlando, they are really very serious about it. Their light-hearted play with words is only superficial, but even this fun disappears when Duke Frederick orders Rosalind to leave his court. Rosalind defends both herself and her father from the duke's accusations of treachery, and Celia comes to the defence of her cousin. We learn from this defence that Rosalind's father was banished many years ago—yet in an earlier scene we were told that the news at court is that 'the old duke is banished by his younger brother the new duke' (1, 1, 91–2). This contradiction is never satisfactorily resolved, and we have to accept that in *As You Like It* there is no real time scale, only 'dramatic time', which can be lengthened or shortened as Shakespeare pleases.

The most powerful motive affecting the duke's action in banishing Rosalind is not a suspicion that she may be a traitor; he has the same reason for hating Rosalind as Oliver has for hating his brother. The duke tells Celia

> Thou art a fool; she robs thee of thy name
> And thou wilt show more bright and seem more virtuous
> When she is gone.　　　　　　　　　　(1, 3, 75–7)

Le Beau told Orlando in the previous scene that Celia was quite unlike her father (1, 2, 245), and now Celia can demonstrate the truth of this.

The decision that Rosalind should dress herself 'all points like a man' (1, 3, 111) would not come as a surprise to Shakespeare's audience. The boy actors who played the women's parts were always ready to get back into their own clothes. Dramatists welcomed this, and enjoyed writing scenes for boys, who were women in disguise—who were boys in women's costumes!

ACT 2

Scene 1 The first Act of the play was an Act of dispersal, bringing to our attention characters who had good reason for being unhappy in the court. This new Act is set in the Forest of Arden (although Scene 2 takes place at court, and Scene 3 outside Oliver's house). The first Scene shows us the realities of the 'golden world' referred to by Charles in *Act 1*, Scene 1. Duke Senior utters the proper sentiments, claiming to find country life much superior to life in 'the envious court' (2, 1, 4). But his suggestion, 'shall we go and kill us venison' (2, 1, 21), makes us aware that this life is not, as we had first supposed, the pastoral existence imagined by poets; in real life, men must eat meat, and they cannot do this without slaughtering the animals.

Jaques, it seems, finds life in the forest much the same as life in town, and we are told of his philosophizing over the wounded deer. But the account is given to us at second hand, not by Jaques himself. By this means Shakespeare lets us know, through the amusement of the duke and his followers, that we are not to take Jaques seriously. When we examine his ideas, we can see that they are not very original, and not very profound, and the excessive emotion of the little episode comes to sound almost comical, with Jaques

> weeping and commenting
> Upon the sobbing deer.   (2, 1, 65–6)

Scene 2 In Scene 2 we return to the court, to learn that Rosalind and Celia have been successful in their plan to run away from the court with Touchstone.

Scene 3 Now Adam takes up the theme of the envy that is aroused in one man at the sight of another man's virtues. His statement of this theme is clear and unmistakable:

> Know you not, master, to some kind of men
> Their graces serve them but as enemies?
> No more do yours: your virtues, gentle master,
> Are sanctified and holy traitors to you.
> O what a world is this when what is comely
> Envenoms him that bears it! (2, 3, 10–15)

By using the words 'sanctified' and 'holy', Adam adds a new, spiritual dimension to the theme: we should remember that Envy is one of the Seven Deadly Sins.

Adam also, by offering his savings to help Orlando, introduces a new theme into the play, and Orlando is quick to state this theme in language as clear as Adam used:

> O good old man, how well in thee appears
> The constant service of the antique world,
> When service sweat for duty not for meed.
> Thou art not for the fashion of these times
> Where none will sweat but for promotion
> And, having that, do choke their service up
> Even with the having. (2, 3, 56–62)

Adam is not really a 'character' at all; he is too symbolic to be life-like. His name immediately suggests the Adam of the Bible, and this suggestion is reinforced by Adam's speeches, which are full of biblical phrases and allusions (2, 3, 43–4, for instance). He is a device which Shakespeare uses to expound certain themes; and he is also necessary to bring out Orlando's tenderness and sense of responsibility later in this Act.

Scene 4   Now Shakespeare begins his exploration of the two sides, male and female, of Rosalind's character. In public, and in all outward appearances, she is masculine—able to take responsibility, to support the weak, and to maintain an appearance of cheerful courage. Privately, underneath the doublet and hose, she is very feminine—longing herself for that support she must appear to give to Celia. Some dramatists contemporary with Shakespeare (such as John Fletcher) disguise their female characters as boys, and then appear to forget that they were first intended to be women. Shakespeare never forgets. Here in *As You Like It* Rosalind's disguise is not only a source of comedy (as we shall see in *Act 3*), but a means by which Shakespeare can present the richness and complexity of Rosalind's character. Conventions of social behaviour in Shakespeare's time—and indeed in England at all times until the present day—would not allow a woman to behave naturally—as an equal—in the company of men. Wit and intelligence were not considered desirable in a lady. As Ganymede, Rosalind is free from social restraint: a theatrical convention of disguise releases her from society's conventions of behaviour.

The fifteen lines of naturalistic prose conversation at the beginning of *Act 2*, Scene 4 are followed by an episode of very formal verse, spoken by the least life-like of all the characters, Silvius. Silvius is taken from literature, not from life. He is typical of the shepherds in romantic pastoral poetry, who live only to love. For an instant, Rosalind joins in Silvius's poetic dream of love:

> Alas, poor shepherd, searching of thy wound,
> I have by hard adventure found mine own.   (2, 4, 40–1)

His patterned verse and her rhyming couplet are both artificial, remote from everyday speech, and we are made aware that there is something comical about this love when Touchstone joins in with a prose account of his own ludicrous love for Jane Smile.

A number of themes have been introduced in the first part of the play, but this scene brings the most important theme, love, which we are to contemplate in various aspects throughout the rest of the play.

Scene 5   In their own part of the Forest the lords, entertained by Amiens' song and the comments of Jaques, are preparing some kind of meal (described in courtly terms as a 'banquet') for the duke. In performance, this meal is perhaps displayed at the back of the stage, so that it is not immediately noticed by Orlando when he brings Adam on stage, exhausted by their wanderings in a strange and uninhabited place.

Scene 6   This short scene reveals another aspect of Orlando, as he tries to cheer and comfort his old servant.

Scene 7   The intellectual discussion between Jaques and Duke Senior on the nature of the satirist and his role in society is one that has no solution: the subject is always topical. It is a matter of opinion, endlessly debatable, whether the satirist should be personally free from reproach, and whether his attack should be directed at a general vice (such as pride) or at an individual instance (one particular proud person).

When Orlando rushes on to the stage, with his sword drawn, the argument stops. Duke Senior reproves Orlando for his unmannerly behaviour, and the mood of the play changes. Once again, in the conversation between Orlando and the duke, court and country life are compared, but this time it is to the advantage of court life. Orlando is proud to say that he is

> inland bred,
> And know some nurture. (2, 7, 97–8)

Now it seems that the duke is not so happy as he claimed to be in *Act 2, Scene 1*; he admits that he and his followers 'have seen better days' (2, 7, 120). Amiens' song tries to re-assert the superiority of country life:

> Blow, blow, thou winter wind,
> Thou art not so unkind
> As man's ingratitude. (2, 7, 174–6)

But the pastoral ideal of the poets has been questioned.

ACT 3

Scene 1 It is odd to hear Duke Frederick, in this short scene, rebuke Oliver for his own most grievous failing—lack of brotherly affection and respect. Now Oliver is sent to find his brother—and he too must go into the Forest.

Scene 2 In a short moonlit interlude, Orlando hangs his poems on a tree, where they hang unseen as

Scene 3 Touchstone and Corin resume their debate on the relative merits of court life and country living. Touchstone is more obviously clever in his debating technique, but the simple arguments put across by Corin seem to win the day. But the poems are quickly found by Rosalind and Celia, and the comedy reaches its height when the two girls read aloud these poetic effusions—which are easily parodied by Touchstone. But Celia contributes her own account of her meeting with Orlando in the Forest, and in excusing her reaction to this news Rosalind once again draws attention to her feminine nature.

> dost thou think, though I am caparisoned like a
> man, I have a doublet and hose in my disposition?
> (3, 3, 173–5)

When it is time for her to speak to Orlando, she can quickly adopt a boyish impertinence and 'speak to him like a saucy lackey' (3, 3, 268).

She draws a picture in words (but see p. 61) of the conventional poetic lover (3, 3, 337–47), and also of the changeable woman in love (365–80). However, at the end of the scene her anxiety that Orlando 'would but call me Rosalind' (3, 3, 382) betrays how deeply she is affected by him.

Scene 4   Another aspect of love is seen when Touchstone attempts to marry Audrey in the Forest. This is the very opposite of Orlando's idealistic emotion. Audrey has never heard the word 'poetical' before, and Touchstone wants to be married in this improper fashion so that,

> not being well married, it will be a good excuse for me hereafter
> to leave my wife.   (3, 3, 78–9)

Scene 5   Alone with Celia, Rosalind does not pretend to be Ganymede; she is a woman, and in love. Celia teases her, and makes fun of Orlando; real love, like Rosalind's, is not afraid of being laughed at.

Scene 6   The love that is now depicted cannot bear laughter. Silvius is the type of lover found only in poetry, who is wholly devoted to his mistress, no matter how cruel she is. Phoebe is probably reading a poem he has written when she says 'Thou tell'st me' (3, 6, 10). It was very common for such lover-poets to speak of the killing glances that came from the lady's cruel eyes. Phoebe examines the metaphor, a poetic 'conceit', and shows how ridiculous it is when taken literally. But Phoebe's criticism is malicious—and it is a fitting punishment that she should herself experience the pangs of love when she is reproached by 'Ganymede'— who will never return her love.

ACT 4

Scene 1   The comedy increases in *Act 4* when Orlando, playing the part of a romantic lover, pleads with Rosalind; she, as Ganymede, adopts an amusingly cynical attitude to love. Suddenly the tone becomes serious, when Rosalind decides that they will 'play' at getting married. This is not all game, and Celia is unwilling to join in—'I cannot say the words' (4, 1, 110). A court of law, in Elizabethan England, would accept this ceremony as a binding contract, committing the lovers to each other, although not permitting them to consummate their union without the blessing of the church. The solemn moment soon passes, and Orlando is not aware of it; but when the teasing and laughter are over, and Orlando has left the stage, Rosalind speaks of her love, with few words and much feeling:

> O coz, coz, coz, my pretty little coz, that thou didst know how
> many fathom deep I am in love! (4, 1, 180–1)

Scene 2

Scene 3

Time passes, with a song; and the comedy is renewed for a moment
when Silvius brings a letter to Rosalind from Phoebe—a letter in which
Phoebe makes use of the same poetic devices that she had scorned in
Act 3, Scene 5. It is a mark of Silvius's love for Phoebe that he is willing
to carry a letter to his rival, but Rosalind despises him, because love has
turned him into a 'tame snake' (4, 3, 68).

A more serious note is introduced by Oliver, telling of his rescue
from death by Orlando. The episode shows Orlando's courage and, even
more important, his generosity, when he had such an opportunity to
repay his brother for Oliver's unnatural hatred of him. And Oliver
himself is the first to acknowledge this

> But kindness, nobler ever than revenge,
> And nature, stronger than his just occasion,
> Made him give battle to the lioness, (4, 3, 125–7)

Rosalind's reaction to Oliver's speech once again forces us to think of
the contrast between her outward appearance as Ganymede, and her
real nature. Oliver does not suspect the truth, but the audience can
enjoy the irony in the words to cheer 'Ganymede':

> Be of good cheer, youth. You a man? You lack a man's heart.
> (4, 3, 161–2)

ACT 5

Scene 1

When Touchstone finds the country lad, William, it is inevitable that he
should make fun of him:

> we that have good wits have much to answer for. We shall be
> flouting; we cannot hold. (5, 1, 11–12)

This scene is necessary, not for anything that it tells us about the plot,
themes, or characters, but to make a natural break between *Act 4*,
Scene 3, and the meeting of Rosalind and Orlando. Also, Robert Armin
(and the actors who have played the part of Touchstone after him)
would enjoy this opportunity to show their wit.

Scene 2

Now it is time for all the lovers to be collected together: the first Act of
this play was an Act of dispersal, and it is balanced here by an Act of

union. With a little surprise, we find that Oliver has joined the band of lovers, because he and Celia, on very short acquaintance, have developed a mutual affection. When Rosalind sees Orlando, for the first time after the fight with the lioness, she tries to laugh at her feelings:

> **Rosalind**
> O, my dear Orlando, how it grieves me to see thee wear thy heart in a scarf.
> **Orlando**
> It is my arm.
> **Rosalind**
> I thought thy heart had been wounded with the claws of a lion.
> **Orlando**
> Wounded it is, but with the eyes of a lady.   (5, 2, 19–24)

Now the conceit does not seem absurd; there is so much true feeling in Rosalind's relationship with Orlando that it is a relief for both of them to hide behind a conventional form of speech. Silvius speaks for all the lovers when he begins a definition of love; the others join in the chorus.

Scene 3   Touchstone and Audrey were absent from this meeting, but they have heard of the wedding-day, and Touchstone tells Audrey

> Tomorrow is the joyful day, Audrey; Tomorrow will we be married.   (5, 3, 1–2)

Once more, a song marks the passage of time.

Scene 4   The final scene of *As You Like It* evokes a mixture of laughter and tears—tears of happiness. After a ritual repetition of the lovers' promises, Touchstone takes centre stage to entertain the other characters (and the audience) while Rosalind, with Celia's help, changes out of her doublet and hose. And when the two girls return they are accompanied by Hymen, the classical god of marriage, who brings the business of the play to a near-supernatural conclusion.

There has always been a magical atmosphere in this imaginary Forest of Arden: good people have found their happiness within its bounds, and one bad character, Oliver, has been converted from his former nature. In *Act 4*, Scene 3, Rosalind asked if he was the man who had tried to kill Orlando, and she received the answer

> 'Twas I, but 'tis not I. I do not shame
> To tell you what I was, since my conversion
> So sweetly tastes, being the thing I am.   (4, 3, 132–4)

With the arrival of Jacques de Boys, we hear what has happened to the other wicked character, the usurping Duke Frederick:

> to the skirts of this wild wood he came,
> Where, meeting with an old religious man,
> After some question with him, was converted
> Both from his enterprise and from the world.   (5, 4, 150–3)

The 'old religious man' belongs to no identifiable religion. The characters in *As You Like It* speak easily in words and phrases from the Bible, as well as referring to the classical gods. The play's action belongs to no particular period, and the Forest of Arden might as well be in France as in Shakespeare's Warwickshire. Neither time nor place is important in this play, and a modern setting is as appropriate for its effects as an attempt at Elizabethan verisimilitude.

The achievement of the play, as we look back from Rosalind's Epilogue, is not simply its creation of an ideal world where the good characters are promised that they will 'live happily ever after', and where bad characters repent of their wickedness and reform their lives. This is what the plot achieves, but *As You Like It* is greater than its plot. The plot provided Shakespeare with a framework, inside which he could arrange themes, points of view, and contrasting attitudes. The final triumph of the play is to have reconciled so many different aspects, so that none dominates at the expense of the others. The various interests, like themes in music, occur and recur through the five Acts, until at the end they, like the characters, have achieved some form of unity within the play's structure and 'Atone together' (5, 4, 102).

Shakespeare's Verse

'God buy you, and you talk in blank verse'

Jaques's satiric comment on Orlando, the romantic young lover, makes us alert to the changes, in *As You Like It*, from prose to verse, and back again. It is usual, in the drama of this period, for the writers to observe a fairly strict rule dividing characters into those who speak verse and those who speak prose. Verse speakers are kings and queens, lords and ladies, and lovers; prose is spoken by comic characters, servants, and country folk. But Shakespeare does not keep to this division in *As You Like It*. In this play it is, broadly speaking, the topic being discussed that decides whether prose or verse should be the medium of discussion: serious matters are spoken of in verse, and prose is used for mundane affairs. For instance—Duke Frederick banishes Rosalind in verse, (*Act 1*, Scene 3), but he watched the wrestling in prose (*Act 1*, Scene 2). When Orlando is explaining his birth and education in the first scene of the play, he speaks in prose; praising Adam's loyalty and industry, his speeches are in verse; comforting his exhausted servant, he returns to prose; and when he appears as the lover of Rosalind, his words naturally fall into the iambic pentameter that Jaques scorns:

> Nay then, God buy you, and you talk in blank verse!   (4, 1, 29)

There is nothing artificial about the line that provokes Jaques's ridicule. The words are common, in everyday use, and they are in their normal order. Without Jaques's comment, we might well not notice that Orlando has delivered a perfect blank verse line:

> Good dáy and háppinéss, dear Rósalínd.   (4, 1, 28)

Blank verse is ideal for English drama because its rhythms are close to those of normal speech; it is capable of infinite variation, yet at the same time it can impose a pattern on the shapelessness of ordinary speech. Basically, the lines, which are unrhymed, are ten syllables long. The syllables have alternating stresses, just like normal English speech; and they divide into five 'feet'.

Duke Frederick
I wóuld thou hádst been són to sóme man élse;
The wórld estéem'd thy fáther hónouráble
But Í did fínd him stíll mine énemý.
Thou shóuldst have bétter pléas'd me wíth this déed
Hadst thóu descénded fróm anóther hóuse.
But fáre thee wéll. Thou árt a gállant yóuth:
I wóuld thou hadst tóld me óf anóther fáther.   *1*, 2, 197–203

Easily the best way to understand and appreciate Shakespeare's verse is to read it aloud—and don't worry if you don't understand everything! Try not to be captivated by the dominant rhythm, but decide which are the most important words in each line and use the regular metre to drive them forward to the listeners.

Source, Date, and Text

Source Shakespeare's main source for *As You Like It* was a popular prose fiction by Thomas Lodge, *Rosalind, or Euphues' Golden Legacy* (1590), which was itself based on a much earlier narrative poem of the fourteenth century—a story of greenwood outlaws and a youngest son who, driven from his father's estate, proves his manhood and virtue in many adventures which include winning a ram in a wrestling match. Lodge adds the more sophisticated elements of a king living as an outlaw in the Forest of Ardennes in France, and the romantic stories of the lovers. His very mannered style, with its elaborate similes and balances, derives from another popular prose romance, John Lyly's *Euphues* (1578), and is occasionally echoed in Shakespeare's play.

Date The play is not mentioned in *Palladis Tamia*, Francis Meres's list of the best contemporary English writing, which was entered for publication in the Stationers' Register in September 1598, but it must have been written before August 1600, when it was registered itself. *As You Like It* could even have been the first play for the new Globe theatre, which probably opened between June and September 1599—so that Jaques's speech about the theatricality of life could become a gesture in the direction of the new motto: *Totus mundus agit histrionem*—all the world plays the actor.

Text Although it was registered in 1600 (probably to frustrate unlawful publication), the play was not published until 1623, in the First Folio of Shakespeare's *Complete Works*, which forms the basis of all modern editions. The present edition uses the text established by Michael Hattaway in 2000 for the New Cambridge Shakespeare.

People in the Play

The household of the late Sir Roland de Boys

Oliver	*the eldest son and heir*
Jacques	*the second son*
Orlando	*the youngest son*
Adam	*a loyal servant to the household*
Denis	Oliver's *servant*

The court of the usurping Duke

Duke Frederick	*the younger brother of* Duke Senior
Celia	*his daughter*
Rosalind	*daughter to* Duke Senior
Le Beau	*a courtier*
Charles	*a wrestler*
Touchstone	*a jester*

The court in exile

Duke Senior

Amiens   *an attendant lord*

Jaques   *a melancholy lord*

The Forest people

Corin   *an old shepherd*

Silvius   *a young shepherd*

Phoebe   *a shepherdess*

William   *a country man*

Audrey   *a country girl*

Sir Oliver Martext   *a country priest*

Hymen   *god of marriage*

Lords, Pages, Foresters, Attendants

'Now Hercules be thy speed, young man.' (*1*, 2, 183) Nancy Carroll as Celia, Alexandra Gilbreath as Rosalind, Joshue Richards as Charles, and Anthony Howell as Orlando, Royal Shakespeare Company, 2001.

ACT 1

Act 1 Scene 1

Sibling rivalry: Orlando decides to leave home to escape the unkindness of a brother who plots his death, and we learn that Duke Senior has been banished from the court by his younger brother.

1 *As I remember*: The scene opens in the middle of a conversation, the characters speaking as they walk downstage towards the audience.

1–2 *it . . . will*: this is the manner it was left to me in (my father's) will.

2 *poor*: a mere.
  crowns: gold coins (worth about 25p in 1600).

3 *charged my brother*: gave the responsibility to my brother.
  on his blessing: as a condition for receiving his blessing.

4 *breed*: educate.

5 *Jacques*: Orlando's second brother does not appear until *Act 5*, Scene 4.
  keeps at school: maintains at university.
  report: rumour.

6 *profit*: progress.

8 *unkept*: without money.

9 *stalling*: stabling.

11 *fair with*: in good condition because of.
  manège: correct paces and conduct.

12 *riders*: trainers.

14 *bound*: indebted.

15–16 *the something . . . me*: my natural social status.

16 *countenance*: behaviour.

17 *hinds*: farm labourers.
  bars: deprives me of.

18 *as . . . lies*: as far as he possibly can.

18–19 *mines my gentility*: undermines my noble birth.

25 *apart*: aside.

25–6 *shake me up*: taunt me.

SCENE 1

Oliver's orchard: enter Orlando *and* Adam

Orlando
As I remember, Adam, it was upon this fashion bequeathed me by will but poor a thousand crowns and, as thou say'st, charged my brother, on his blessing, to breed me well: and there begins my sadness. My
5 brother Jacques he keeps at school, and report speaks goldenly of his profit. For my part, he keeps me rustically at home or, to speak more properly, stays me here at home unkept—for call you that 'keeping' for a gentleman of my birth, that differs not from the stalling
10 of an ox? His horses are bred better for, besides that they are fair with their feeding, they are taught their manège, and to that end riders dearly hired. But I, his brother, gain nothing under him but growth—for the which his animals on his dunghills are as much bound to him as I.
15 Besides this nothing that he so plentifully gives me, the something that Nature gave me his countenance seems to take from me: he lets me feed with his hinds, bars me the place of a brother, and, as much as in him lies, mines my gentility with my education. This is it, Adam, that
20 grieves me, and the spirit of my father, which I think is within me, begins to mutiny against this servitude. I will no longer endure it, though yet I know no wise remedy how to avoid it.

Enter Oliver

Adam
Yonder comes my master, your brother.
Orlando
25 Go apart, Adam, and thou shalt hear how he will shake me up.

Adam *withdraws*

Oliver
Now, sir, what make you here?
Orlando
Nothing: I am not taught to make anything.
Oliver
What mar you then, sir?
Orlando
30 Marry, sir, I am helping you to mar that which God
made, a poor unworthy brother of yours, with idleness.
Oliver
Marry, sir, be better employed, and be naught awhile.
Orlando
Shall I keep your hogs and eat husks with them? What
prodigal portion have I spent that I should come to
35 such penury?
Oliver
Know you where you are, sir?
Orlando
O, sir, very well: here in your orchard.
Oliver
Know you before whom, sir?
Orlando
Aye, better than him I am before knows me: I know you
40 are my eldest brother, and in the gentle condition of
blood you should so know me. The courtesy of nations
allows you my better in that you are the first-born, but
the same tradition takes not away my blood, were there
twenty brothers betwixt us. I have as much of my father
45 in me as you, albeit I confess your coming before me is
nearer to his reverence.
Oliver
[*Raising his hand*] What, boy!
Orlando
[*Seizing his brother*] Come, come, elder brother, you are
too young in this.
Oliver
50 Wilt thou lay hands on me, villain?
Orlando
I am no villein: I am the youngest son of Sir Roland de

27 *what make you*: what are you doing;
Orlando deliberately mistakes *make* =
construct.

30 *Marry*: by St Mary (a mild oath).

32 *be naught awhile*: get away with you
(a common catchphrase).

33–5 *Shall . . . penury*: Orlando refers to
Jesus's parable of the prodigal son
who wasted his inheritance ('portion')
and was forced to eat the scraps
('husks') on which the pigs were fed
(Luke 15:11–32).

39, 41 *know*: acknowledge.
40–1 *in . . . blood*: because of our noble
breeding.
41 *courtesy of nations*: custom among
civilized people.
42 *allows*: acknowledges.
43 *blood*: breeding.

45–6 *your . . . reverence*: being born
before me entitles you to more of the
respect due to him.

47 *boy*: An insult that provokes Orlando
to demonstrate unexpected strength.

49 *in this*: in strength.

50 *thou*: Oliver's use of the familiar
pronoun (instead of 'you') is insulting.
villain: rogue; Orlando hears a pun on
'villein' (= peasant).

Boys; he was my father, and he is thrice a villain that says such a father begot villeins. Wert thou not my brother, I would not take this hand from thy throat till this other
55 had pulled out thy tongue for saying so: thou hast railed on thyself.

Adam

[*Coming forward*] Sweet masters, be patient, for your father's remembrance, be at accord.

Oliver

Let me go, I say.

Orlando

60 I will not till I please. You shall hear me. My father charged you in his will to give me good education: you have trained me like a peasant, obscuring and hiding from me all gentleman-like qualities. The spirit of my father grows strong in me—and I will no longer endure
65 it. Therefore allow me such exercises as may become a gentleman or give me the poor allottery my father left me by testament: with that I will go buy my fortunes.

He releases Oliver

Oliver

And what wilt thou do? Beg when that is spent? Well, sir, get you in. I will not long be troubled with you: you
70 shall have some part of your 'will'; I pray you leave me.

Orlando

I will no further offend you than becomes me for my good.

Oliver

[*To* Adam] Get you with him, you old dog.

Adam

Is 'old dog' my reward? Most true, I have lost my teeth in
75 your service. God be with my old master: he would not have spoke such a word.

[*Exeunt* Orlando *and* Adam

Oliver

Is it even so, begin you to grow upon me? I will physic your rankness, and yet give no thousand crowns neither.—Holla, Denis.

55–6 *railed on thyself*: slandered yourself (by saying that his father could beget a villain).

58 *at accord*: at peace.

63 *qualities*: accomplishments.

65 *exercises*: pursuits.
may become: may be suited to.
66 *allottery*: share of the inheritance.
67 *testament*: will.

70 *your 'will'*: what you want.

77 *grow upon me*: become a nuisance to me.
physic: cure, purge.
78 *rankness*: excessive wild growth.

Enter Denis

Denis

80 Calls your worship?

Oliver

Was not Charles, the duke's wrestler, here to speak with me?

Denis

83 *So please you*: if it may please you.
importunes: demands.

So please you, he is here at the door, and importunes access to you.

Oliver

85 Call him in.   [*Exit* Denis

86 *'Twill . . . is*: Oliver speaks *aside*, to himself.

'Twill be a good way, and tomorrow the wrestling is.

Enter Charles

Charles

87 *morrow*: morning.

Good morrow to your worship.

Oliver

Good Monsieur Charles, what's the new news at the new court?

Charles

90 *old news*: Celia says (*1*, 3, 66) that at the time of the duke's exile she was too young to appreciate Rosalind's worth.
91 *old duke*: i.e. Duke Senior.

90 There's no news at the court, sir, but the old news: that is, the old duke is banished by his younger brother, the new duke, and three or four loving lords have put themselves into voluntary exile with him, whose lands and revenues enrich the new duke; therefore he gives

95 *good leave*: full permission.

95 them good leave to wander.

Oliver

Can you tell if Rosalind, the duke's daughter, be banished with her father?

Charles

O no; for the duke's daughter, her cousin, so loves her, being ever from their cradles bred together, that she

99 *bred*: brought up.
100 *to stay*: if she were forced to stay.

100 would have followed her exile or have died to stay behind her; she is at the court and no less beloved of her uncle than his own daughter, and never two ladies loved as they do.

Oliver

Where will the old duke live?

allusion *not gave to poor* *from rich &*

Charles

105 They say he is already in the Forest of Arden, and a
many merry men with him; and there they live like the
old Robin Hood of England. They say many young
gentlemen flock to him every day, and fleet the time
carelessly as they did in the golden world.

Oliver   *pastoral allusion*

110 What, you wrestle tomorrow before the new duke?

Charles

Marry, do I, sir; and I came to acquaint you with a
matter. I am given, sir, secretly to understand that your
younger brother Orlando hath a disposition to come in,
disguised, against me to try a fall. Tomorrow, sir, I

115 wrestle for my credit, and he that escapes me without
some broken limb shall acquit him well. Your brother is
but young and tender and, for your love, I would be
loath to foil him, as I must for my own honour, if he
come in; therefore, out of my love to you, I came hither

120 to acquaint you withal, that either you might stay him
from his intendment, or brook such disgrace well as he
shall run into, in that it is a thing of his own search and
altogether against my will.

Oliver

Charles, I thank thee for thy love to me, which thou

125 shalt find I will most kindly requite. I had myself notice
of my brother's purpose herein, and have by underhand
means laboured to dissuade him from it—but he is
resolute. I'll tell thee, Charles, it is the stubbornest
young fellow of France, full of ambition, an envious

130 emulator of every man's good parts, a secret and
villainous contriver against me, his natural brother.
Therefore use thy discretion: I had as lief thou didst
break his neck as his finger. And thou wert best look
to't—for if thou dost him any slight disgrace or if he do

135 not mightily grace himself on thee, he will practise
against thee by poison, entrap thee by some treacherous
device, and never leave thee till he hath ta'en thy life by
some indirect means or other. For I assure thee—and
almost with tears I speak it—there is not one so young

140 and so villainous this day living. I speak but brotherly of

---

105 *Forest of Arden*: an extensive tract of wild countryside near Stratford-upon-Avon, Shakespeare's birthplace; various references, however, suggest that the play, like its source, might be set in France—see 'Source, Date, and Text', p.xxv.
105–6 *a many*: a lot of.
107 *Robin . . . England*: A romantic outlaw of English folklore.
108 *fleet*: pass away.
109 *carelessly*: free from care.
golden world: the first age of the world.
113 *disposition*: inclination.
114 *disguised*: It was not appropriate for a gentleman to fight with a common wrestler.
fall: bout.
115 *credit*: reputation.
117 *love*: sake.
118 *foil*: overthrow.

120 *withal*: with this.
120–1 *stay . . . intendment*: stop him from carrying out his intentions.
121 *brook*: endure.

125 *kindly requite*: appropriately reward.
126–7 *by . . . means*: unobtrusively.

129 *of France*: See above, 105 note.
129–30 *envious emulator*: malicious detractor.
130 *parts*: qualities.
131 *contriver*: plotter.
natural: blood.
132 *had as lief*: would rather.
133–4 *look to't*: be careful.
135 *grace . . . thee*: distinguish himself against you.
135–6 *practise . . . poison*: plot to kill you with poison.

140 *brotherly*: as a brother, i.e. not objectively.

141 *anatomize*: explain in every detail (the word is used particularly to refer to the dissecting of corpses).

144 *his payment*: what he deserves.
go alone: walk unaided (without crutches).

147 *stir this gamester*: provoke this fighter: Oliver speaks scornfully of his brother.

150–1 *of all sorts*: by all ranks.
enchantingly: as though they were under his spell.
152 *people*: servants.
153 *misprized*: despised.
154 *clear all*: solve all problems.
155 *kindle*: stir up, incite.
boy: a final insult.

Act 1 Scene 2
Rosalind and Celia try to persuade Orlando not to risk his life in a wrestling-match, but his determination and skill overcome the professional fighter—and conquer Rosalind's heart.

1 *thee*: Celia, as the ruling duke's daughter, uses the familiar form of address to Rosalind, who replies with the more formal 'you'.
sweet my coz: my sweet cousin.
2 *I show . . . of*: I appear happier than I really am.
3 *would . . . merrier*: do you want me to seem even happier; many editors emend to 'yet I were'.
4 *learn*: teach.
5 *remember*: think about.
8 *so*: provided that.
9 *take*: accept.

11 *righteously tempered*: properly composed.

---

him, but should I anatomize him to thee as he is, I must blush and weep, and thou must look pale and wonder.

Charles

I am heartily glad I came hither to you. If he come tomorrow, I'll give him his payment; if ever he go alone 145 again, I'll never wrestle for prize more—and so God keep your worship. [*Exit*

Oliver

Farewell, good Charles.—Now will I stir this gamester. I hope I shall see an end of him, for my soul—yet I know not why—hates nothing more than he. Yet he's gentle, 150 never schooled and yet learned, full of noble device, of all sorts enchantingly beloved, and indeed so much in the heart of the world, and especially of my own people who best know him, that I am altogether misprized. But it shall not be so long this wrestler shall clear all: 155 nothing remains but that I kindle the boy thither, which now I'll go about. [*Exit*

Scene 2

The garden of the Duke's palace: enter Rosalind and Celia

Celia

I pray thee, Rosalind, sweet my coz, be merry.

Rosalind

Dear Celia, I show more mirth than I am mistress of, and would you yet were merrier: unless you could teach me to forget a banished father, you must not learn me 5 how to remember any extraordinary pleasure.

Celia

Herein, I see, thou lov'st me not with the full weight that I love thee; if my uncle, thy banished father, had banished thy uncle, the duke my father, so thou hadst been still with me, I could have taught my love to take 10 thy father for mine; so wouldst thou, if the truth of thy love to me were so righteously tempered as mine is to thee.

13 *estate*: situation.
15–16 *nor none . . . have*: and is not likely to have any more.
17 *perforce*: by force.
18 *render*: return.
23 *Marry*: by the Virgin Mary.
I prithee: I pray you.
withal: with it.
24 *in good earnest*: seriously.
25 *with . . . blush*: without more damage than an innocent blush.
26 *come off*: retire from.
28–30 *Let . . . equally*: The goddess Fortune was traditionally represented as blindfolded, controlling a wheel which turned from happiness to despair—but Celia's comparison domesticates her and her spinning-wheel.

28 *housewife*: a) mistress of the house; b) hussy, whore. The word is pronounced 'hussif'.
31 *would*: wish.
34 *scarce*: rarely.
35 *honest*: virtuous.
36 *ill-favouredly*: unattractively.

37 *office*: function.
38 *reigns . . . world*: commands material possessions.
39 *lineaments of Nature*: natural qualities (such as virtue, wit, beauty).
39s.d *Enter . . . clown*: Touchstone probably wears the 'motley' (= multicoloured) dress of a professional jester.

Rosalind
Well, I will forget the condition of my estate to rejoice in yours.
Celia
15 You know my father hath no child but I, nor none is like to have; and, truly, when he dies thou shalt be his heir: for what he hath taken away from thy father perforce I will render thee again in affection. By mine honour, I will, and when I break that oath, let me turn monster.
20 Therefore, my sweet Rose, my dear Rose, be merry.
Rosalind
From henceforth I will, coz, and devise sports. Let me see, what think you of falling in love?
Celia
Marry, I prithee do, to make sport withal: but love no man in good earnest—nor no further in sport
25 neither—than with safety of a pure blush thou mayst in honour come off again.
Rosalind
What shall be our sport then?
Celia
Let us sit and mock the good housewife Fortune from her wheel, that her gifts may henceforth be bestowed
30 equally.
Rosalind
I would we could do so: for her benefits are mightily misplaced, and the bountiful blindwoman doth most mistake in her gifts to women.
Celia
'Tis true, for those that she makes fair she scarce makes
35 honest, and those that she makes honest she makes very ill-favouredly.
Rosalind
Nay, now thou goest from Fortune's office to Nature's: Fortune reigns in gifts of the world, not in the lineaments of Nature.

Enter Touchstone *the clown*

'Mistress, you must come away to your father.' (*1*, 2, 53) Adrian Schiller as Touchstone, Royal Shakespeare Company, 2000.

Celia

40 No? When Nature hath made a fair creature, may she
not by Fortune fall into the fire? Though Nature hath
given us wit to flout at Fortune, hath not Fortune sent
in this fool to cut off the argument?

Rosalind

Indeed there is Fortune too hard for Nature, when
45 Fortune makes Nature's natural the cutter-off of
Nature's wit.

Celia

Peradventure this is not Fortune's work neither but
Nature's who, perceiving our natural wits too dull to
reason of such goddesses, hath sent this natural for our
50 whetstone: for always the dullness of the fool is the
whetstone of the wits.—How now, Wit, whither wander
you?

Touchstone

Mistress, you must come away to your father.

Celia

Were you made the messenger?

Touchstone

55 No, by mine honour, but I was bid to come for you.

Rosalind

Where learned you that oath, fool?

Touchstone   *insightful but funny*

Of a certain knight that swore, by his honour, they were
good pancakes, and swore, by his honour, the mustard
was naught. Now, I'll stand to it, the pancakes were
60 naught and the mustard was good—and yet was not the
knight forsworn.

Celia

How prove you that in the great heap of your
knowledge?

Rosalind

Ay, marry, now unmuzzle your wisdom.

Touchstone

65 Stand you both forth now. Stroke your chins and swear,
by your beards, that I am a knave.

Celia

By our beards—if we had them—thou art.

---

good but good play for confusion

41 *by Fortune . . . fire*: by chance lose
her virtue.
42 *wit*: intelligence.
flout at: mock.

45 *natural*: fool, idiot.
46 *Nature's wit*: i.e. their conversation.

47 *Peradventure*: perhaps.

50 *whetstone*: stone for sharpening
knives.

59 *naught*: bad, rubbish.
stand to it: swear.
61 *was . . . forsworn*: the knight had not
perjured himself.

69 *that that is not*: that which does not exist (in this case, their beards).

71 *sworn it away*: i.e. by breaking oaths.

73 *Prithee*: I pray you.

76 *taxation*: slander.

80 *troth*: faith.
80–1 *since . . . silenced*: Celia may be alluding to a decree of June 1599 prohibiting the printing of satires and epigrams.
82–3 *'Monsieur Le Beau'*: Celia appears to be drawing attention to the character's foppish behaviour and affected diction.

85 *put*: force.

87 *marketable*: easy to sell (because plumper).
88 *Bonjour*: good day; Celia is perhaps encouraging the courtier's affectation (but *see 1, 1, 105 note*).
89 *lost*: missed.

90 *colour*: kind.

Touchstone
By my knavery—if I had it—then I were. But if you
swear by that that is not you are not forsworn: no more
70 was this knight swearing by his honour, for he never
had any; or if he had, he had sworn it away before ever
he saw those pancakes or that mustard.
Celia
Prithee, who is't that thou mean'st?
Touchstone
One that old Frederick, your father, loves.
Celia
75 My father's love is enough to honour him. Enough!
Speak no more of him; you'll be whipped for taxation
one of these days.
Touchstone
The more pity that fools may not speak wisely what
wise men do foolishly.
Celia
80 By my troth, thou say'st true: for, since the little wit that
fools have was silenced, the little foolery that wise men
have makes a great show.—Here comes 'Monsieur the
Beau'.

Enter Le Beau

Rosalind
With his mouth full of news.
Celia
85 Which he will put on us as pigeons feed their young.
Rosalind
Then shall we be news-crammed.
Celia
All the better: we shall be the more marketable.—
Bonjour, Monsieur Le Beau, what's the news?
Le Beau
Fair princess, you have lost much good sport.
Celia
90 'Sport': of what colour?
Le Beau
'What colour', madam? How shall I answer you?

93 *Destinies*: the Fates, the three Greek
   goddesses who ruled over the life of
   man.
94 *trowel*: a bricklayer's instrument for
   spreading plaster. Celia approves
   Touchstone's exaggerated imitation of
   Le Beau's formal speech.
95 *rank*: position (as a witty fool).
96 *loosest . . . smell*: release your usual
   fart; Rosalind puns on *rank* = stink.

97 *amaze*: confuse.

101 *yet to do*: still to be done.

105 *an old tale*: The single parent with
    three children is a common subject in
    popular fiction (including
    Shakespeare's *King Lear*).
106 *proper*: fine.
107 *presence*: appearance.

108 *bills*: notices, writings.
108–9 *Be . . . presents*: The opening words
    of many public documents: Rosalind
    puns on *presents* = writings.

111 *which*: the same.

115 *dole*: lamentation.

Rosalind
As wit and fortune will.
   Touchstone
[*Imitating* Le Beau] Or as the destinies decrees.
   Celia
Well said: that was laid on with a trowel.
   Touchstone
95 Nay, if I keep not my rank—
   Rosalind
Thou loosest thy old smell.
   Le Beau
You amaze me, ladies! I would have told you of good
wrestling which you have lost the sight of.
   Rosalind
Yet tell us the manner of the wrestling.
   Le Beau
100 I will tell you the beginning and, if it please your
ladyships, you may see the end, for the best is yet to do;
and here where you are they are coming to perform it.
   Celia
Well, the beginning that is dead and buried.
   Le Beau
There comes an old man and his three sons—
   Celia
105 I could match this beginning with an old tale.
   Le Beau
Three proper young men, of excellent growth and
presence—
   Rosalind
With bills on their necks: 'Be it known unto all men by
these presents'.
   Le Beau
110 The eldest of the three wrestled with Charles, the duke's
wrestler, which Charles in a moment threw him and
broke three of his ribs that there is little hope of life in
him. So he served the second and so the third: yonder
they lie, the poor old man, their father, making such
115 pitiful dole over them that all the beholders take his part
with weeping.
   Rosalind
Alas!

[handwritten note: rank = position or smell; play on words]

Touchstone

But what is the sport, monsieur, that the ladies have lost?

Le Beau

120 Why, this that I speak of.

Touchstone

Thus men may grow wiser every day. It is the first time that ever I heard breaking of ribs was sport for ladies.

Celia

123 *promise*: assure.

Or I, I promise thee.

Rosalind

124 *broken music*: a) music arranged for more than one instrument; b) rib-cracking.

But is there any else longs to see this broken music in his
125 sides? Is there yet another dotes upon rib-breaking? Shall we see this wrestling, cousin?

Le Beau

You must if you stay here, for here is the place appointed for the wrestling and they are ready to perform it.

Celia

130 Yonder, sure, they are coming. Let us now stay and see it.

130s.d. *Flourish*: trumpet fanfare.

Flourish. Enter Duke Frederick, Lords, Orlando, Charles, *and* Attendants

Duke Frederick

131–2 *his own . . . forwardness*: his own recklessness is responsible for the danger he is in.

Come on; since the youth will not be entreated, his own peril on his forwardness.

Rosalind

Is yonder the man?

Le Beau

Even he, madam.

Celia

135 *successfully*: able to succeed.

135 Alas, he is too young; yet he looks successfully.

Duke Frederick

136 *cousin*: The word could describe a variety of relationships.
are . . . hither: have you sneaked in here.
138 *liege*: lord.

How now, daughter—and cousin: are you crept hither to see the wrestling?

Rosalind

Aye, my liege, so please you give us leave.

Duke Frederick

140 *odds*: inequality.

You will take little delight in it, I can tell you: there is
140 such odds in the man. In pity of the challenger's youth,

141 *fain*: gladly.

142 *move*: persuade.

148 *general challenger*: challenger who
will take on all opponents.
come but: merely enter the
competition.

153 *fear . . . adventure*: fearfulness of your
undertaking.

157–8 *your . . . misprized*: your reputation
will not be dishonoured by this.
158 *suit*: plea.
159 *go forward*: proceed.

160 *with . . . thoughts*: by thinking badly
of me.
161 *wherein*: in respect of which.

164 *foiled*: overthrown.
gracious: favoured by Fortune.

166 *friends*: kinsfolk.

168 *supplied*: occupied.

I would fain dissuade him, but he will not be entreated.
Speak to him, ladies: see if you can move him.

Celia

Call him hither, good Monsieur Le Beau.

Duke Frederick

Do so; I'll not be by.

The Duke *stands aside*

Le Beau

145 Monsieur the challenger, the princess calls for you.

Orlando

I attend them with all respect and duty.

Rosalind

Young man, have you challenged Charles the wrestler?

Orlando

No, fair princess, he is the general challenger. I come but
in as others do to try with him the strength of my youth.

Celia

150 Young gentleman, your spirits are too bold for your
years: you have seen cruel proof of this man's strength.
If you saw yourself with your eyes or knew yourself with
your judgement, the fear of your adventure would
counsel you to a more equal enterprise. We pray you, for
155 your own sake, to embrace your own safety and give
over this attempt.

Rosalind

Do, young sir: your reputation shall not therefore be
misprized. We will make it our suit to the duke that the
wrestling might not go forward.

Orlando

160 I beseech you, punish me not with your hard thoughts,
wherein I confess me much guilty to deny so fair and
excellent ladies anything. But let your fair eyes and
gentle wishes go with me to my trial, wherein if I be
foiled, there is but one shamed that was never gracious;
165 if killed, but one dead that is willing to be so. I shall do
my friends no wrong, for I have none to lament me; the
world no injury, for in it I have nothing; only in the
world I fill up a place, which may be better supplied
when I have made it empty.

170 *would*: wish.

171 *eke*: stretch.

172 *be . . . in you*: underestimate your strength.

174–5 *to lie with*: a) to be buried in; b) to have sexual intercourse with.

176 *modest*: a) humble; b) decent. *working*: endeavour.

178 *warrant*: assure.

182 *come your ways*: let's get on with it.

183 *Hercules*: the superman of classical mythology. *be thy speed*: give you success.

187 *a thunderbolt . . . eye*: It was a popular conceit of romantic love poetry to claim Jove's power for the eyes of a mistress (see *3*, 6, 10).
188 *down*: be thrown down.

Rosalind
170 The little strength that I have, I would it were with you.
     Celia
     And mine to eke out hers.
     Rosalind
     Fare you well: pray heaven I be deceived in you.
     Celia
     Your heart's desires be with you.
     Charles
     Come, where is this young gallant that is so desirous to
175 lie with his mother earth?
     Orlando
     Ready, sir, but his will hath in it a more modest working.
     Duke Frederick
     You shall try but one fall.
     Charles
     No, I warrant your grace you shall not entreat him to a
     second, that have so mightily persuaded him from a
180 first.
     Orlando
     You mean to mock me after: you should not have
     mocked me before. But come your ways.
     Rosalind
     Now Hercules be thy speed, young man.
     Celia
     I would I were invisible, to catch the strong fellow by the
185 leg.

     They wrestle

     Rosalind
     O excellent young man.
     Celia
     If I had a thunderbolt in mine eye, I can tell who should
     down.

     Charles *is thrown to the ground. Shout*

     Duke Frederick
     No more, no more!

190 *breathed*: warmed-up.

192 *He cannot speak*: Probably Orlando
has not killed but foiled the wrestler
with some clever trick (see *2, 2, 14*).

*hi
my pencil is in
the best
position right
now*

197 *I would . . . else*: Duke Frederick
changes the emotional tone of the
scene when he begins to speak in
verse.
199 *still*: always.
200 *Thou shouldst*: you would.
201 *house*: family.

hello

206 *change that calling*: exchange that
name.

209 *was . . . mind*: share my father's
opinion.

211 *unto*: as well as.

214 *envious*: malicious.
215 *Sticks . . . heart*: wounds me to the
heart.

Orlando
190 Yes, I beseech your grace, I am not yet well breathed.
Duke Frederick
How dost thou, Charles?
Le Beau *le beau*
He cannot speak, my lord.
Duke Frederick
Bear him away.
                                            [Charles *is carried out*
What is thy name, young man?
Orlando
195 Orlando, my liege, the youngest son of Sir Roland de
Boys.
Duke Frederick
I would thou hadst been son to some man else;
The world esteem'd thy father honourable
But I did find him still mine enemy.
200 Thou shouldst have better pleas'd me with this deed
Hadst thou descended from another house.
But fare thee well. Thou art a gallant youth:
I would thou hadst told me of another father.
                [*Exeunt* Duke Frederick, Le Beau, Touchstone,
                                    Lords, *and* Attendants
Celia
Were I my father, coz, would I do this?
Orlando
205 I am more proud to be Sir Roland's son—
His youngest son—and would not change that calling
To be adopted heir to Frederick.
Rosalind
My father lov'd Sir Roland as his soul
And all the world was of my father's mind;
210 Had I before known this young man his son,
I should have given him tears unto entreaties
Ere he should thus have ventur'd.
Celia
                                            Gentle cousin,
Let us go thank him and encourage him;
My father's rough and envious disposition
215 Sticks me at heart.—Sir, you have well deserv'd:
If you do keep your promises in love

'Gentleman, Wear this for me' (*1*, 2, 219–20). Alexandra Gilbreath as Rosalind and Anthony Howell as Orlando, Royal Shakespeare Company, 2000.

217 *But justly*: exactly.

But justly, as you have exceeded all promise,
Your mistress shall be happy.
    Rosalind
[*Giving him a chain from her neck*] Gentleman,

220 *out of suits*: out of favour.

221 *could*: would like to.
   hand: power.

220 Wear this for me: one out of suits with Fortune,
That could give more, but that her hand lacks
    means.—
Shall we go, coz?
    Celia
                Aye.—Fare you well, fair gentleman.

They turn to go

223 *better parts*: spirits.

    Orlando
[*Aside*] Can I not say, 'I thank you'? My better parts
Are all thrown down, and that which here stands up

225 *quintain*: target used by riders 'tilting'
in tournaments (see illustration).
mere: completely.

225 Is but a quintain, a mere lifeless block.
    Rosalind
[*To Celia*] He calls us back. My pride fell with my
    fortunes,
I'll ask him what he would.—Did you call, sir?
Sir, you have wrestled well and overthrown
More than your enemies.

They gaze upon each other

227 *would*: wants.
230 *Have with you*: I'm coming.

    Celia
                Will you go, coz?
    Rosalind
230 Have with you.—Fare you well.
              [*Exeunt* Rosalind *and* Celia
    Orlando
What passion hangs these weights upon my tongue?
I cannot speak to her, yet she urg'd conference.

232 *urg'd conference*: invited
conversation.

Enter Le Beau

234 *Or*: either.

O poor Orlando! thou art overthrown:
Or Charles or something weaker masters thee.

238 *condition*: mood.
239 *misconsters*: misconstrues,
 misinterprets.
240 *humorous*: temperamental;
 Elizabethan medical theory taught
 that every body was composed of four
 elements (earth, air, fire, and water)
 which gave rise to four 'humours' or
 temperaments.
 indeed: in reality.
241 *More . . . conceive*: would be better
 for you to imagine.

246 *taller*: more finely dressed: Rosalind
 describes herself as 'more than
 common tall' (*1*, 3, 110).

249 *whose loves*: their love to each other.

252 *gentle*: well born.
253 *Grounded*: based.
 argument: reason.

256 *on my life*: I'll bet my life on it.

258 *world*: time.
259 *knowledge*: friendship.

260 *bounden*: indebted.

261 *smother*: slow-burning fire; 'Shunning
 the smoke, he fell into the fire'
 (proverbial).

Le Beau

235 Good sir, I do in friendship counsel you
 To leave this place. Albeit you have deserv'd
 High commendation, true applause, and love,
 Yet such is now the duke's condition
 That he misconsters all that you have done.
240 The duke is humorous: what he is indeed
 More suits you to conceive than I to speak of.

Orlando

I thank you, sir; and pray you tell me this:
 Which of the two was daughter of the duke,
 That here was at the wrestling?

Le Beau

245 Neither his daughter, if we judge by manners,
 But yet indeed the taller is his daughter;
 The other is daughter to the banish'd duke
 And here detain'd by her usurping uncle
 To keep his daughter company, whose loves
250 Are dearer than the natural bond of sisters.
 But I can tell you that of late this duke
 Hath ta'en displeasure 'gainst his gentle niece,
 Grounded upon no other argument
 But that the people praise her for her virtues
255 And pity her for her good father's sake;
 And, on my life, his malice 'gainst the lady
 Will suddenly break forth. Sir, fare you well,
 Hereafter, in a better world than this,
 I shall desire more love and knowledge of you.

Orlando

260 I rest much bounden to you: fare you well.

[*Exit* Le Beau

Thus must I from the smoke into the smother,
 From tyrant duke unto a tyrant brother.
 But heavenly Rosalind!   [*Exit*

Act 1 Scene 3
Rosalind takes Celia into her confidence,
but Duke Frederick banishes Rosalind from
his court. Together the girls plan to disguise
themselves and escape into the forest.

1 *Cupid*: the classical god of love.

3 *to throw . . . dog*: A proverbial
expression.

8–9 *mad without any*: crazy (for love)
beyond all reason.

11 *my child's father*: the man who should
father my child—i.e. Orlando.
12 *briars*: thorn-bushes, difficulties.
working-day: everyday, ordinary.
13 *burs*: a) seed-heads of prickly plants;
b) throat-tickles.
13–14 *holy-day foolery*: festival fun.

16 *coat*: petticoat, skirt.

18 *Hem*: cough.

19 *cry 'hem'*: attract his attention with a
cough.

21 *take the part*: support.
22 *a good . . . you*: bless you.
22–3 *try . . . fall*: chance a bout (of love)
even though you may lose by it.
23 *turning . . . service*: setting aside
these jokes (as servants dismissed
from their jobs).
24 *in good earnest*: seriously.

SCENE 3

Duke Frederick's *palace: enter* Celia *and* Rosalind

Celia
Why, cousin; why, Rosalind—Cupid have mercy, not a
word?
Rosalind
Not one to throw at a dog.
Celia
No, thy words are too precious to be cast away upon
5 curs: throw some of them at me. Come, lame me with
reasons.
Rosalind
Then there were two cousins laid up, when the one
should be lamed with reasons, and the other mad
without any.
Celia
10 But is all this for your father?
Rosalind
No, some of it is for my child's father—O how full of
briars is this working-day world!
Celia
They are but burs, cousin, thrown upon thee in holy-
day foolery: if we walk not in the trodden paths, our
15 very petticoats will catch them.
Rosalind
I could shake them off my coat: these burs are in my
heart.
Celia
Hem them away.
Rosalind
I would try, if I could cry 'hem' and have him.
Celia
20 Come, come, wrestle with thy affections.
Rosalind
O they take the part of a better wrestler than myself.
Celia
O, a good wish upon you: you will try in time in despite
of a fall. But turning these jests out of service, let us talk
in good earnest. Is it possible, on such a sudden, you

29 *kind of chase*: course of argument.
30 *dearly*: keenly.

31 *faith*: in truth.

32 *deserve well*: merit my hatred
(according to this line of reasoning).

33 *for that*: i.e. because her father loved
his father.

36 *Mistress*: The Duke speaks with
contempt—and again his rage
changes the tone (and form) of the
scene.
dispatch . . . haste: get away as
quickly as you can with safety.
37 *cousin*: kinswoman.

39 *public court*: area of jurisdiction.

41 *fault*: offence.
bear: take.
42–3 *If . . . desires*: if I understand
myself, or know what I want.
44 *frantic*: mad.

25 should fall into so strong a liking with old Sir Roland's
youngest son?
Rosalind
The duke my father loved his father dearly.
Celia
Doth it therefore ensue that you should love his son
dearly? By this kind of chase I should hate him for my
30 father hated his father dearly; yet I hate not Orlando.
Rosalind
No, faith, hate him not, for my sake.
Celia
Why should I not? Doth he not deserve well?

Enter Duke Frederick *with* Lords

Rosalind
Let me love him for that, and do you love him because I
do. Look, here comes the duke.
Celia
35 With his eyes full of anger.
Duke Frederick
Mistress, dispatch you with your safest haste
And get you from our court.
Rosalind
                                    Me, uncle?
Duke Frederick
                                    You, cousin.
Within these ten days if that thou be'st found
So near our public court as twenty miles,
40 Thou diest for it.
Rosalind
                        I do beseech your grace
Let me the knowledge of my fault bear with me:
If with myself I hold intelligence,
Or have acquaintance with mine own desires,
If that I do not dream or be not frantic
45 (As I do trust I am not) then, dear uncle,
Never so much as in a thought unborn,
Did I offend your highness.

Duke Frederick

Thus do all traitors:

48 *purgation*: action of clearing themselves.

If their purgation did consist in words,

They are as innocent as grace itself.

50 *suffice thee*: be enough for you.

50 Let it suffice thee that I trust thee not.

Rosalind

Yet your mistrust cannot make me a traitor;

52 *whereon*: on what grounds.

Tell me whereon the likelihoods depends?

Duke Frederick

Thou art thy father's daughter, there's enough.

Rosalind

So was I when your highness took his dukedom,

55 So was I when your highness banish'd him;

Treason is not inherited, my lord,

57 *friends*: family.

Or if we did derive it from our friends,

58 *What's that*: what does that matter.

What's that to me? My father was no traitor.

59 *good my liege*: my good lord.

Then, good my liege, mistake me not so much

60 *my poverty is treacherous*: that because I am poor I am a traitor.

60 To think my poverty is treacherous.

Celia

Dear sovereign, hear me speak.

Duke Frederick

Aye, Celia, we stay'd her for your sake,

62 *stay'd*: kept.

Else had she with her father rang'd along.

63 *with . . . along*: wandered off together with (alongside) her father.

Celia

I did not then entreat to have her stay,

65 *remorse*: pity.

65 It was your pleasure—and your own remorse.

66 *too young*: Compare *1*, *1*, *90*.

I was too young that time to value her,

But now I know her: if she be a traitor,

68 *still*: always.

Why so am I. We still have slept together,

69 *at an instant*: at the same moment. *eat*: eaten.

Rose at an instant, learn'd, play'd, eat together,

70 *Juno's swans*: In classical mythology it is usually Venus whose chariot is drawn by swans (but occasionally the gods might share their attributes).

70 And wheresoe'er we went, like Juno's swans,

Still we went coupled and inseparable.

72 *subtle*: cunning. *smoothness*: deceptive charm.

Duke Frederick

She is too subtle for thee, and her smoothness,

Her very silence, and her patience

Speak to the people and they pity her.

75 *name*: reputation.

75 Thou art a fool: she robs thee of thy name

And thou wilt show more ~~bright and seem~~ more virtuous

When she is gone.

Celia starts to speak

                Then open not thy lips!
Firm and irrevocable is my doom
Which I have pass'd upon her: she is banish'd.
    Celia
80 Pronounce that sentence then on me, my liege,
I cannot live out of her company.
    Duke Frederick
You are a fool.—You, niece, provide yourself:
If you outstay the time, upon mine honour
And in the greatness of my word, you die.
                 [Exeunt Duke *and* Lords
    Celia
85 O my poor Rosalind, whither wilt thou go?
Wilt thou change fathers? I will give thee mine!
I charge thee be not thou more griev'd than I am.
    Rosalind
I have more cause.
    Celia
                Thou hast not, cousin:
Prithee be cheerful. Know'st thou not the duke
90 Hath banish'd me, his daughter?
    Rosalind
                   That he hath not.
    Celia
No? 'Hath not'? Rosalind lacks then the love
Which teacheth thee that thou and I am one;
Shall we be sunder'd, shall we part, sweet girl?
No, let my father seek another heir!
95 Therefore devise with me how we may fly,
Whither to go, and what to bear with us;
And do not seek to take your change upon you,
To bear your griefs yourself and leave me out:
For, by this heaven, now at our sorrows pale,
100 Say what thou canst, I'll go along with thee.
    Rosalind
Why, whither shall we go?
    Celia
To seek my uncle in the Forest of Arden.

78 *doom*: sentence.

84 *greatness*: power.

87 *charge*: order, request.

89 *Prithee*: I pray you.

92 *thou . . . one*: 'A friend is one's second self' (proverbial).
am: The verb agrees with 'I', the nearer subject.
93 *sunder'd*: separated.

97 *change*: change of fortune.

99 *at . . . pale*: dimmed in sympathy with our grief.

Rosalind

Alas, what danger will it be to us

(Maids as we are) to travel forth so far?

105 Beauty provoketh thieves sooner than gold.

Celia

I'll put myself in poor and mean attire

And with a kind of umber smirch my face;

The like do you. So shall we pass along

And never stir assailants.

Rosalind

Were it not better,

110 Because that I am more than common tall,

That I did suit me all points like a man,

A gallant curtal-axe upon my thigh,

A boar-spear in my hand, and in my heart

Lie there what hidden woman's fear there will.

115 We'll have a swashing and a martial outside

As many other mannish cowards have

That do outface it with their semblances.

Celia

What shall I call thee when thou art a man?

Rosalind

I'll have no worse a name than Jove's own page,

120 And therefore look you call me 'Ganymede'.

But what will you be call'd?

Celia

Something that hath a reference to my state:

No longer 'Celia' but 'Aliena'.

Rosalind

But, cousin, what if we assay'd to steal

125 The clownish fool out of your father's court:

Would he not be a comfort to our travail?

Celia

He'll go along o'er the wide world with me:

Leave me alone to woo him. Let's away

And get our jewels and our wealth together,

130 Devise the fittest time and safest way

To hide us from pursuit that will be made

After my flight. Now go in we content,

To liberty, and not to banishment.   [*Exeunt*

---

106 *mean*: lowly.

107 *umber*: a brown paint (which would make the white-skinned court ladies look like peasants). *smirch*: stain.

108 *The like do you*: you do the same.

109 *stir*: provoke.

110 *common*: usually.

111 *suit me all points*: dress myself in every way.

112 *curtle-axe*: cutlass (a short sword).

115 *swashing*: swaggering. *outside*: appearance.

116 *mannish cowards*: cowardly men.

117 *outface it*: brazen it out. *semblances*: appearances.

120 *Ganymede*: a beautiful youth who was snatched up by Jupiter to become the god's cup-bearer.

123 *Aliena*: a name meaning 'the stranger'.

124 *assay'd*: attempted.

126 *travail*: wearisome journey.

128 *woo*: coax.

'Are not these woods More free from peril than the envious court?' (2, 1, 3–4) Ian Hogg as Duke Senior and Paul Ewing as Amiens, Royal Shakespeare Company, 2000.

ACT 2

Os.d. *foresters*: forest-dwellers; the appearance of these characters establishes the location of the scene.
1 *co-mates*: companions.
2 *old*: old-established; 'Custom makes all things easy' (proverbial).
3 *painted pomp*: artificial splendour.
4 *envious*: malicious.
5 *the . . . Adam*: the hardship suffered by all people since Adam (the first man).
6 *as*: such as.
7 *churlish*: rude, violent.
11 *feelingly*: by experience.
persuade: impress upon.
12 *Sweet . . . adversity*: 'Adversity makes men wise' (proverbial).
13–14 *the toad . . . head*: Toads, popularly supposed to be poisonous, were also thought to carry a precious stone in their heads as antidote to the poison.

15 *exempt . . . haunt*: free from interruption by other people.
20 *style*: a) manner of expression; b) way of living.
21 *venison*: deer; these could only be taken with permission from the king.
22 *irks*: distresses.
dappled fools: simple parti-coloured creatures.
23 *burghers*: citizens.
24 *confines*: territory.
forked heads: forked; arrows.

SCENE 1

The Forest of Arden: enter Duke Senior, Amiens, *and two or three* Lords *dressed as foresters*

Duke Senior
Now, my co-mates and brothers in exile,
Hath not old custom made this life more sweet
Than that of painted pomp? Are not these woods
More free from peril than the envious court?
5 Here feel we not the penalty of Adam,
The seasons' difference, as the icy fang
And churlish chiding of the winter's wind—
Which when it bites and blows upon my body
Even till I shrink with cold, I smile and say,
10 'This is no flattery'—these are counsellors
That feelingly persuade me what I am.
Sweet are the uses of adversity
Which like the toad, ugly and venomous,
Wears yet a precious jewel in his head,
15 And this our life exempt from public haunt
Finds tongues in trees, books in the running brooks,
Sermons in stones, and good in everything.
Amiens
I would not change it; happy is your grace
That can translate the stubbornness of Fortune
20 Into so quiet and so sweet a style.
Duke Senior
Come, shall we go and kill us venison?
And yet it irks me the poor dappled fools,
Being native burghers of this desert city,
Should, in their own confines, with forked heads
25 Have their round haunches gor'd.
First Lord
Indeed, my lord.

26 *melancholy*: morose, world-weary; the affectation of this 'humour' (see *1, 2, 240 note*), was fashionable at the time.
   'Jaques': the French name, pronounced with two syllables, was adopted by some Englishmen to show they had been abroad.
27 *in that kind*: accordingly.
30 *along*: stretched out—a characteristic melancholic pose.
31 *antique*: ancient.
32 *brawls*: chatters, runs noisily.
33 *sequester'd*: separated from the herd.

39 *Cours'd*: chased.
40 *piteous*: pitiful.
41 *marked of*: markèd; observed by. *Jaques*: The rhythm indicates pronunciation as a single syllable, punning on the word 'jakes' (= privy).
43 *Augmenting*: adding to.

44 *moralize*: give a moral interpretation to.
45 *similes*: comparisons.
46 *needless*: not in need.
47 *testament*: will.
48 *worldlings*: people devoted to worldly objects.
   sum of more: excessive possessions.
50 *of*: by.
   velvet friend: i.e. the stag, carrying the 'velvet' covering of new antlers.
51 *part*: separate from.
52 *flux*: constant stream.
   anon: presently.
   careless: carefree.
53 *Full . . . pasture*: well-fed by grazing.
54 *stays*: pauses.
56 *'Tis . . . fashion*: that's exactly how it is.

61 *mere*: absolute.
   what's worse: whatever is worse than these.
62 *kill them up*: exterminate them.
63 *assign'd . . . place*: natural habitat.

The melancholy 'Jaques' grieves at that,
And in that kind swears you do more usurp
Than doth your brother that hath banish'd you.
Today my lord of Amiens and myself
30 Did steal behind him as he lay along
Under an oak, whose antique root peeps out
Upon the brook that brawls along this wood,
To the which place a poor sequester'd stag,
That from the hunter's aim had ta'en a hurt,
35 Did come to languish; and indeed, my lord,
The wretched animal heav'd forth such groans
That their discharge did stretch his leathern coat
Almost to bursting, and the big round tears
Cours'd one another down his innocent nose
40 In piteous chase; and thus the hairy fool,
Much marked of the melancholy Jaques,
Stood on th'extremest verge of the swift brook,
Augmenting it with tears.

Duke Senior
                                   But what said Jaques?
Did he not moralize this spectacle?

First Lord
45 O yes, into a thousand similes.
First, for his weeping in the needless stream:
'Poor deer,' quoth he, 'thou mak'st a testament
As worldlings do, giving thy sum of more
To that which hath too much.' Then, being there alone,
50 Left and abandoned of his velvet friend:
''Tis right,' quoth he, 'thus misery doth part
The flux of company.' Anon a careless herd,
Full of pasture, jumps along by him
And never stays to greet him. 'Aye,' quoth Jaques,
55 'Sweep on, you fat and greasy citizens,
'Tis just the fashion. Wherefore do you look
Upon that poor and broken bankrupt there?'
Thus most invectively he pierceth through
The body of country, city, court,
60 Yea, and of this our life, swearing that we
Are mere usurpers, tyrants, and what's worse,
To fright the animals and to kill them up
In their assign'd and native dwelling place.

Duke Senior

And did you leave him in this contemplation?

Second Lord

65 We did, my lord, weeping and commenting

Upon the sobbing deer.

Duke Senior

         Show me the place;

I love to cope him in these sullen fits,

For then he's full of matter.

First Lord

           I'll bring you to him straight.

               [*Exeunt*

65 *commenting*: meditating.

67 *cope*: debate with.

68 *matter*: ideas.
 straight: immediately.

SCENE 2

Act 2 Scene 2
Duke Frederick organizes a search for his
daughter.

Duke Frederick's palace: enter Duke Frederick *with*
Lords

Duke Frederick

Can it be possible that no man saw them?

It cannot be: some villeins of my court

Are of consent and sufferance in this.

First Lord

I cannot hear of any that did see her;

5 The ladies, her attendants of her chamber,

Saw her abed and, in the morning early,

They found the bed untreasur'd of their mistress.

Second Lord

My lord, the roinish clown, at whom so oft

Your grace was wont to laugh, is also missing.

10 Hisperia, the princess' gentlewoman

Confesses that she secretly o'erheard

Your daughter and her cousin much commend

The parts and graces of the wrestler

That did but lately foil the sinewy Charles;

15 And she believes, wherever they are gone,

That youth is surely in their company.

Duke Frederick

Send to his brother: 'Fetch that gallant hither.'

If he be absent, bring his brother to me—

I'll make him find him. Do this suddenly,

2 *villeins*: a) servants, peasants;
 b) wrongdoers.
3 *Are . . . this*: are accessories who have
 allowed this to happen.

6 *abed*: in bed.
7 *untreasur'd*: robbed.

8 *roinish*: scurvy (covered with scale),
 base.
9 *wont*: accustomed.

13 *parts*: qualities.
14 *foil*: defeat.

17 *gallant*: fine gentleman (he speaks
 sarcastically of Orlando).

19 *suddenly*: at once.

20 *inquisition*: enquiry.
   quail: give up.
21 *bring again*: bring back.

Act 2 Scene 3
Orlando must escape from his brother, and
Adam volunteers his service.

2 *memory*: reminder.

4 *what make you*: what are you doing.

7 *fond*: foolish.

8 *bonny*: strong.
   prizer: prizefighter.
   humorous: moody (see note to
   1, 2, 240).

12 *No more do yours*: your virtues do no
   more for you (i.e. they are your
   enemies).
14 *comely*: becoming, praiseworthy.
15 *Envenoms*: poisons.

23 *use to lie*: usually sleep.

25 *cut you off*: kill you.
26 *practices*: plots.

---

20 And let not search and inquisition quail
   To bring again these foolish runaways.   [*Exeunt*

SCENE 3

Outside Oliver's *house: enter* Orlando

Orlando
Who's there?

Enter Adam

Adam
What, my young master! O my gentle master,
O my sweet master, O you memory
Of old Sir Roland, why, what make you here?
5 Why are you virtuous? Why do people love you?
And wherefore are you gentle, strong, and valiant?
Why would you be so fond to overcome
The bonny prizer of the humorous duke?
Your praise is come too swiftly home before you.
10 Know you not, master, to some kind of men
Their graces serve them but as enemies?
No more do yours: your virtues, gentle master,
Are sanctified and holy traitors to you.
O what a world is this when what is comely
15 Envenoms him that bears it!
Orlando
Why, what's the matter?
Adam
                          O unhappy youth,
Come not within these doors: within this roof
The enemy of all your graces lives
Your brother—no, no brother—yet the son—
20 Yet not the son, I will not call him son
Of him I was about to call his father—
Hath heard your praises, and this night he means
To burn the lodging where you use to lie
And you within it. If he fail of that,
25 He will have other means to cut you off:
I overhead him and his practices.

27 *no place*: no place for you, no home.
   butchery: slaughterhouse.

30 *so*: provided that.

32 *boisterous*: unruly, violent.
33 *common*: public.

35 *do . . . can*: whatever happens to me.
37 *diverted blood*: unnatural blood
   relationship.
   bloody: bloodthirsty, murderous.
38 *crowns*: gold coins; four crowns = £1
   (half the annual wage of a
   servingman).
39 *thrifty hire*: wages saved by thrift.
40 *to . . . nurse*: to care for me.
41 *service*: the ability to serve.
42 *unregarded . . . thrown*: as an old man
   I should be thrown aside and not
   noticed.
43 *He . . . feed*: God 'giveth to the beast
   his food, and to the young ravens
   which cry', Psalm 147:9.
44 *providently . . . sparrow*: 'Are not five
   sparrows sold for two farthings, and
   not one of them is forgotten before
   God', Luke 12:6.
   providently: providentially.
47 *lusty*: vigorous, healthy.
49 *rebellious*: causing rebellion of the
   body.
50 *unbashful forehead*: cheeky
   impudence.
51 *The . . . debility*: Adam may be
   referring modestly to sexual
   intercourse, which was said to weaken
   a man.
52 *lusty*: bracing.
53 *Frosty*: Adam perhaps describes his
   white hair or beard.
57 *constant*: faithful.
   antique: ancient.
58 *service*: servants.
   sweat: worked.
   meed: reward, bribe.
61–2 *choke . . . having*: withdraw their
   labour as soon as they get their
   promotion.

This is no place, this house is but a butchery:
Abhor it, fear it, do not enter it.
    Orlando
Why whither, Adam, wouldst thou have me go?
    Adam
30 No matter whither, so you come not here.
    Orlando
What, wouldst thou have me go and beg my food,
Or with a base and boisterous sword enforce
A thievish living on the common road?
This I must do or know not what to do;
35 Yet this I will not do, do how I can.
I rather will subject me to the malice
Of a diverted blood and bloody brother.
    Adam
But do not so: I have five hundred crowns,
The thrifty hire I sav'd under your father,
40 Which I did store to be my foster-nurse
When service should in my old limbs lie lame
And unregarded age in corners thrown;
Take that, and He that doth the ravens feed,
Yea providently caters for the sparrow,
45 Be comfort to my age. Here is the gold:
All this I give you; let me be your servant—
Though I look old, yet I am strong and lusty;
For in my youth I never did apply
Hot and rebellious liquors in my blood,
50 Nor did not with unbashful forehead woo
The means of weakness and debility;
Therefore my age is as a lusty winter,
Frosty but kindly. Let me go with you:
I'll do the service of a younger man
55 In all your business and necessities.
    Orlando
O good old man, how well in thee appears
The constant service of the antique world,
When service sweat for duty not for meed.
Thou art not for the fashion of these times
60 Where none will sweat but for promotion
And, having that, do choke their service up
Even with the having. It is not so with thee;

But, poor old man, thou prun'st a rotten tree
That cannot so much as a blossom yield,
65   In lieu of all thy pains and husbandry.
But come thy ways: we'll go along together
And, ere we have thy youthful wages spent,
We'll light upon some settled low content.
   Adam
Master, go on, and I will follow thee
70   To the last gasp with truth and loyalty.
From seventeen years till now almost fourscore
Here liv'd I, but now live here no more.
At seventeen years many their fortunes seek,
But at fourscore it is too late a week;
75   Yet Fortune cannot recompense me better
Than to die well and not my master's debtor.

                                                      [*Exeunt*

SCENE 4

The forest: enter Rosalind *in man's attire as*
Ganymede, Celia *as a shepherdess* Aliena, *and the*
clown Touchstone *in the costume of a retainer*

   Rosalind
O Jupiter, how merry are my spirits!
   Touchstone
I care not for my spirits, if my legs were not weary.
   Rosalind
[*Aside*] I could find in my heart to disgrace my man's
apparel and to cry like a woman; but I must comfort the
5   weaker vessel, as doublet and hose ought to show itself
courageous to petticoat; therefore—courage, good
Aliena!
   Celia
I pray you bear with me, I cannot go no further.
   Touchstone
For my part, I had rather bear with you than bear you;
10   yet I should bear no cross if I did bear you, for I think
you have no money in your purse.
   Rosalind
Well, this is the Forest of Arden.

Glosses (left column):

65   *In lieu of*: in return for.
      pains: cares.
      husbandry: good management.
66   *come thy ways*: come along.
67   *youthful*: earned in youth.
68   *light upon*: find.
      settled low content: steady and
      humble way of life.
69   *thee*: encouraged by Orlando's
      response, Adam now addresses him in
      the familiar form.

74   *too . . . week*: far too late.

Act 2 Scene 4
Rosalind and Celia meet Silvius and
arrange to buy a cottage.

1   *Jupiter*: Rosalind, assuming a false
      cheerfulness and entering into the role
      of Ganymede (see *1*, *3*, *120*), invokes
      the aid of Jupiter, who was noted for
      his 'jovial' disposition.
3 s.d. *[Aside]*: Rosalind might speak
      these lines either '*Aside*' or directly to
      Touchstone.
5   *weaker vessel*: A proverbial phrase: a
      husband should give honour to his
      wife, 'as unto the weaker vessel'
      (1 Peter 3:7).
      doublet and hose: jacket and close-
      fitting breeches.

10   *cross*: a) burden; b) silver coin
      stamped with a cross.

Opposite of pastoral conventions ↓

Touchstone

13 *now . . . am I*: I am a bigger fool now
that I am in Arden.

Aye, now am I in Arden, the more fool I! When I was at
home I was in a better place; but travellers must be
15 content.

Enter Corin *and* Silvius

Rosalind
Aye, be so, good Touchstone. Look you who comes
here:
A young man and an old in solemn talk.
    Corin
That is the way to make her scorn you still.
    Silvius
O Corin, that thou knew'st how I do love her.
    Corin

20 *partly*: to some extent.

20 I partly guess, for I have lov'd ere now.
    Silvius
No, Corin, being old, thou canst not guess, *ageist*

21 *Though*: even though.
23 *a midnight pillow*: a pillow at
midnight.
24 *like to*: similar to.

Though in thy youth thou wast as true a lover
As ever sigh'd upon a midnight pillow.
But if thy love were ever like to mine—
25 As sure I think did never man love so—
How many actions most ridiculous

27 *to*: into.
fantasy: affections.

Hast thou been drawn to by thy fantasy?
    Corin
Into a thousand that I have forgotten.
    Silvius
O thou didst then never love so heartily.
30 If thou remembrest not the slightest folly
That ever love did make thee run into,
Thou hast not lov'd.
Or if thou hast not sat as I do now,

34 *Wearing*: exhausting.
in . . . praise: by praising your
mistress.

Wearing thy hearer in thy mistress' praise,
35 Thou hast not lov'd.
Or if thou hast not broke from company
Abruptly as my passion now makes me,
Thou hast not lov'd.
O Phoebe, Phoebe, Phoebe!   [*Exit*

'I pray you, one of you question yond man' (*2*, 4, 58). Joe Melia as Touchstone, Susan Fleetwood as Rosalind, Tom Wilkinson as Corin, and Sinead Cusack as Celia, Royal Shakespeare Company, 1980.

Rosalind

40 *searching*: probing.

41 *hard adventure*: bad luck.

42–3 *broke . . . stone*: Touchstone's anecdote probably has bawdy overtones: 'sword' and 'stone' = penis and testicle.
45 *batler*: wooden beater used for washing clothes.
dugs: teats.
46 *peasecod*: pea plant.
47 *cods*: peapods.

49 *capers*: actions.
50–1 *as . . . folly*: as all that lives must die, so all who love must act foolishly.

52 *Thou . . . of*: you know.

57 *something*: somewhat.

58 *yond*: yonder.

61 *clown*: country fellow, fool.

65 *Else*: otherwise.

66 *Good even*: The expression was used any time after noon.

Rosalind
40 Alas, poor shepherd, searching of thy wound,
   I have by hard adventure found mine own.
   Touchstone
   And I mine: I remember when I was in love, I broke my
   sword upon a stone and bid him take that for coming
   a-night to Jane Smile; and I remember the kissing of her
45 batler and the cow's dugs that her pretty chapped hands
   had milked; and I remember the wooing of a peasecod
   instead of her, from whom I took two cods and, giving
   her them again, said with weeping tears, 'Wear these for
   my sake.' We that are true lovers run into strange capers;
50 but as all is mortal in Nature, so is all nature in love
   mortal in folly.
   Rosalind
   Thou speak'st wiser than thou art ware of.
   Touchstone
   Nay, I shall ne'er be ware of mine own wit till I break my
   shins against it.
   Rosalind
55 Jove, Jove, this shepherd's passion
   Is much upon my fashion.
   Touchstone
   And mine, but it grows something stale with me.
   Celia
   I pray you, one of you question yond man
   If he for gold will give us any food:
60 I faint almost to death.
   Touchstone
   Holla, you, clown!
   Rosalind
   Peace, fool; he's not thy kinsman.
   Corin
   Who calls?
   Touchstone
   Your betters, sir.
   Corin
65 Else are they very wretched.
   Rosalind
   [*To* Touchstone] Peace, I say.—Good even to you,
   friend.

Corin
And to you, gentle sir, and to you all.
    Rosalind
I prithee, shepherd, if that love or gold
Can in this desert place buy entertainment,
70 Bring us where we may rest ourselves and feed.
Here's a young maid with travel much oppress'd
And faints for succour.
    Corin
               Fair sir, I pity her
And wish, for her sake more than for mine own,
My fortunes were more able to relieve her;
75 But I am shepherd to another man,
And do not shear the fleeces that I graze.
My master is of churlish disposition
And little recks to find the way to heaven
By doing deeds of hospitality.
80 Besides, his cot, his flocks, and bounds of feed
Are now on sale, and at our sheepcote now
By reason of his absence there is nothing
That you will feed on. But what is, come see,
And in my voice most welcome shall you be.
    Rosalind
85 What is he that shall buy his flock and pasture?
    Corin
That young swain that you saw here but erewhile,
That little cares for buying anything.
    Rosalind
I pray thee, if it stand with honesty,
Buy thou the cottage, pasture, and the flock,
90 And thou shalt have to pay for it of us.
    Celia
And we will mend thy wages. I like this place
And willingly could waste my time in it.
    Corin
Assuredly the thing is to be sold.
Go with me. If you like upon report
95 The soil, the profit, and this kind of life,
I will your very faithful feeder be,
And buy it with your gold right suddenly.   [*Exeunt*

---

68 *if that*: if.
69 *entertainment*: hospitality.

71 *oppress'd*: exhausted.
72 *faints for succour*: is becoming weak for want of aid.

76 *shear . . . graze*: get the wool from the sheep I look after.
77 *churlish*: miserly.
78 *recks*: cares.

80 *cot*: cottage.
bounds of feed: pasture land.
81 *on sale*: being sold.

83 *what is*: what there is.
84 *in my voice*: as far as I can say.

86 *swain*: lover.
but erewhile: just a short time ago.

88 *if . . . honesty*: if you can do it honestly.

90 *have to pay*: have what is necessary to pay.

91 *mend*: improve.
92 *waste*: spend.

94 *upon report*: when you hear more of it.

96 *feeder*: shepherd.
97 *right suddenly*: without delay.

Act 2 Scene 5
Amiens sings while preparing a banquet for
the Duke.

SCENE 5

The forest: enter Amiens, Jaques, *and others:* Lords
dressed as foresters

Song

Amiens
    Under the greenwood tree,
    Who loves to lie with me
    And turn his merry note
    Unto the sweet bird's throat:

5   Come hither, come hither, come hither:
      Here shall he see
      No enemy
    But winter and rough weather.

Jaques
More, more, I prithee more.

Amiens
10 It will make you melancholy, Monsieur Jaques.

Jaques
I thank it. More, I prithee more: I can suck melancholy
out of a song as a weasel sucks eggs. More, I prithee
more.

Amiens
My voice is ragged: I know I cannot please you.

Jaques
15 I do not desire you to please me, I do desire you to sing.
Come, more, another stanzo—call you 'em 'stanzos'?

Amiens
What you will, Monsieur Jaques.

Jaques
Nay, I care not for their names; they owe me nothing.
Will you sing?

Amiens
20 More at your request than to please myself.

Jaques
Well then, if ever I thank any man, I'll thank you; but
that they call 'compliment' is like th'encounter of two
dog-apes. And when a man thanks me heartily,

1 *greenwood*: wood or forest in leaf.
2 *Who*: whoever.
3 *turn*: tune.

10 *melancholy*: Music was often
associated with romantic melancholy.

12 *as . . . eggs*: The weasel, a creature
noted for ferocity, sometimes steals
eggs from birds' nests.

14 *ragged*: hoarse.
16 *stanzo*: stanza; Jaques mocks the
newfangled word.

22 *that*: that which.
'*compliment*': courtesy.
23 *dog-apes*: dog-faced baboons.

25 *the beggarly thanks*: the extravagant thanks of a beggar.

27 *cover the while*: meanwhile, lay out a cloth for the meal.

29 *look you*: look for you.

31 *disputable*: argumentative (see 2, 1, 67–8).
matters: topics.

methinks I have given him a penny and he renders me

25 the beggarly thanks. Come, sing; and you that will not, hold your tongues.

Amiens

Well, I'll end the song.—Sirs, cover the while; the duke will drink under this tree.—He hath been all this day to look you.

Jaques

30 And I have been all this day to avoid him: he is too disputable for my company: I think of as many matters as he, but I give heaven thanks and make no boast of them. Come, warble, come.

Song. All together here

        Who doth ambition shun
35   And loves to live i'th'sun;
        Seeking the food he eats
        And pleas'd with what he gets:

        Come hither, come hither, come hither:
            Here shall he see
40   No enemy
        But winter and rough weather.

Jaques

I'll give you a verse to this note that I made yesterday in despite of my invention.

42 *note*: tune.
42–3 *in . . . invention*: without using my imagination.

Amiens

And I'll sing it.

Jaques

45 Thus it goes:
        If it do come to pass
        That any man turn ass,
        Leaving his wealth and ease,
        A stubborn will to please,

50 *Ducdame*: The word is probably meaningless.

53 *And if*: if.

50   Ducdame, ducdame, ducdame:
            Here shall he see
            Gross fools as he,
        And if he will come to me.

Amiens

What's that 'ducdame'?

56 *rail against*: verbally abuse.
56–7 *all . . . Egypt*: They were all slain by
the Angel of Death when Pharaoh
refused to free the Israelites
(Exodus 11:5)—but the point of the
remark is not clear.
58 *banquet*: a light meal of fruit, sweets,
and wine; this meal is probably set
out at the back of the stage, where
Orlando and Adam will not be aware
of it.

Act 2 Scene 6
Orlando comforts the exhausted Adam.

4 *heart*: courage.

5 *comfort*: take comfort.

6 *uncouth*: strange, uncultivated.
anything savage: any wild animal.
7 *conceit*: imagination.

9 *comfortable*: comforted, cheerful.
the arm's end: at arm's length.
10 *presently*: immediately.

13 *Well said*: Adam probably makes some
inarticulate response.
cheerly: cheerfully.

16 *desert*: lonely place.

Jaques
55 'Tis a Greek invocation to call fools into a circle. I'll go
sleep if I can: if I cannot, I'll rail against all the first-born
of Egypt.
　　Amiens
And I'll go seek the duke: his banquet is prepared.
　　　　　　　　　　　　　　　　　　　　　　[Exeunt

SCENE 6

The forest: enter Orlando *and* Adam

　　Adam
Dear master, I can go no further. O, I die for food. Here
lie I down and measure out my grave. Farewell, kind
master.
　　Orlando
Why, how now, Adam, no greater heart in thee? Live a
5 little, comfort a little, cheer thyself a little. If this
uncouth forest yield anything savage, I will either be
food for it or bring it for food to thee. Thy conceit is
nearer death than thy powers. For my sake be
comfortable; hold death a while at the arm's end. I will
10 here be with thee presently, and if I bring thee not
something to eat, I will give thee leave to die; but if thou
diest before I come, thou art a mocker of my labour.
Well said, thou look'st cheerly, and I'll be with thee
quickly. Yet thou liest in the bleak air. Come, I will bear
15 thee to some shelter, and thou shalt not die for lack of a
dinner if there live anything in this desert. Cheerly,
good Adam.　　　　　　　　　　　　　　　　*[Exeunt*

Act 2 Scene 7
Conversation is interrupted when Orlando
breaks into the gathering of Duke Senior
and his lords, but he is received with
courtesy and kindness.

0s.d. *outlaws*: the exiled lords are
   outside the law and deprived of its
   protection.

2 *like*: in the shape of.

3 *but even now*: just at this moment.

5 *compact of jars*: made up of discords.

6 *discord . . . spheres*: discord in the
   heavens; according to Pythagoras, the
   planets ('spheres') generated perfect
   harmony as they revolved.
11 *merrily*: An unfamiliar condition for
   Jaques.
13 *A motley fool*: a professional jester;
   Jaques seems to have recognized
   Touchstone's style even though he has
   discarded his distinctive costume (see
   2, 4, 0 s.d.).
   a miserable world: Jaques replies to
   the Duke's question (9–10).
16 *rail'd on*: abused.
17 *set terms*: rhetorical eloquence.
18 *quoth*: said.
19 *fortune*: wealth; 'Fortune favours fools'
   (proverbial).
20 *dial*: pocket sun-dial, watch.
   poke: wallet.

21 *lack-lustre*: dull, dreary.
23 *wags*: goes.

SCENE 7

The forest banquet. Enter Duke Senior, Amiens, *and*
Lords *like outlaws*

Duke Senior
I think he be transform'd into a beast,
For I can nowhere find him like a man.
   Amiens
My lord, he is but even now gone hence;
Here was he merry, hearing of a song.
   Duke Senior
5 If he, compact of jars, grow musical,
We shall have shortly discord in the spheres.
Go seek him; tell him I would speak with him.

Enter Jaques

   Amiens
He saves my labour by his own approach.
   Duke Senior
Why, how now, monsieur, what a life is this
10 That your poor friends must woo your company?
What, you look merrily?
   Jaques
A fool, a fool: I met a fool i'th'forest,
A motley fool—a miserable world—
As I do live by food, I met a fool
15 Who laid him down and bask'd him in the sun
And rail'd on Lady Fortune in good terms,
In good set terms, and yet a motley fool.
'Good morrow, fool,' quoth I. 'No, sir,' quoth he,
'Call me not fool till heaven hath sent me fortune.'
20 And then he drew a dial from his poke
And looking on it, with lack-lustre eye,
Says, very wisely, 'It is ten o'clock.
Thus we may see,' quoth he, 'how the world wags:
'Tis but an hour ago since it was nine,
25 And after one hour more 'twill be eleven;
And so, from hour to hour, we ripe and ripe,
And then, from hour to hour, we rot and rot,

29 *moral*: moralize.

30 *Chanticleer*: A traditional name for a cock, found in Chaucer's 'Nun's Priest's Tale'.

31 *deep-contemplative*: profoundly philosophical.

32 *sans*: without.

34 *motley's . . . wear*: a fool's costume is the only one to wear.

36–42 *one . . . forms*: Jaques's savage attack on Touchstone's laboured wit is apparently unprovoked.

39–40 *remainder . . . voyage*: ship's bread left over after a voyage.

40 *places*: subjects, topics.

41 *observation*: knowledge, information. *vents*: utters.

44 *suit*: a) request; b) costume; c) offshoot (the pronunciation 'shoot' leads to the subsequent word-play).

45 *weed*: a) clear; b) clothe.

46 *rank*: excessively.

48 *Withal*: as well. *as large . . . wind*: a licence as free as the wind.

49 *blow on*: attack, criticize.

50 *galled*: gallèd; hurt.

52 *why*: reason.

53–5 *He . . . bob*: someone who has been cleverly ridiculed by a fool is very silly if he appears not to appreciate the joke ('bob'), even though he has been stung by it.

56 *anatomiz'd*: laid bare.

57 *squand'ring glances*: random satirical hits.

58 *Invest*: robe.

59–61 *I will . . . medicine*: Jaques offers to perform the traditional function of the satirist in purging a sick world of its folly.

62 *Fie on thee*: don't be silly.

And thereby hangs a tale.' When I did hear
The motley fool thus moral on the time,
30 My lungs began to crow like Chanticleer
That fools should be so deep-contemplative;
And I did laugh, sans intermission,
An hour by his dial. O noble fool,
O worthy fool: motley's the only wear.
    Duke Senior
35 What fool is this?
    Jaques
A worthy fool: one that hath been a courtier
And says, 'If ladies be but young and fair,
They have the gift to know it'; and in his brain,
Which is as dry as the remainder biscuit
40 After a voyage, he hath strange places cramm'd
With observation, the which he vents
In mangled forms. O that I were a fool!
I am ambitious for a motley coat.
    Duke Senior
Thou shalt have one.
    Jaques
                    It is my only suit,
45 Provided that you weed your better judgements
Of all opinion that grows rank in them
That I am wise. I must have liberty
Withal, as large a charter as the wind,
To blow on whom I please: for so fools have.
50 And they that are most galled with my folly,
They most must laugh. And why, sir, must they so?
The why is plain as way to parish church:
He that a fool doth very wisely hit,
Doth very foolishly, although he smart,
55 If he seem senseless of the bob. If not,
The wise man's folly is anatomiz'd
Even by the squand'ring glances of the fool.
Invest me in my motley; give me leave
To speak my mind, and I will through and through
60 Cleanse the foul body of th'infected world,
If they will patiently receive my medicine.
    Duke Senior
Fie on thee! I can tell what thou wouldst do.

63   *counter*: in exchange for a worthless token.

64   *Most . . . sin*: 'He finds fault with others and does worse himself' (proverbial).

65–9 *For . . . world*: The Duke is probably suspicious of the well-travelled Jaques.

66   *brutish sting*: animal lust.

67   *embossed*: embossèd; swollen. *headed evils*: evils that have come to a head (like boils).

68   *free foot*: utter (and immoral) freedom.

69   *disgorge*: vomit. *general*: whole.

70–1 *who . . . party*: Disregarding the Duke's charges, Jaques continues with the justification of satire.

70   *cries out on*: denounces.

71   *tax*: accuse. *private party*: individual person.

73   *the weary . . . ebb*: the basic resources, exhausted, dry up.

75–6 *the city-woman . . . shoulders*: a citizen's wife dresses like royalty.

76   *cost*: expense, extravagance. *unworthy*: plebeian, lowly.

77   *in*: forward.

78   *such . . . neighbour*: her neighbour is just the same.

79   *of basest function*: in the most humble employment.

80   *his . . . cost*: his finery is not paid for by me (and is therefore none of my business).

81   *therein*: in saying this. *suits*: matches.

82   *mettle*: spirit, nature.

84   *right*: justice.

85   *free*: innocent.

86   *taxing*: criticism.

90   *necessity*: need.

91   *Of . . . of*: what sort of cocky young man is this.

Jaques
What, for a counter, would I do but good?
   Duke Senior
Most mischievous foul sin in chiding sin:
65 For thou thyself hast been a libertine,
As sensual as the brutish sting itself,
And all th'embossed sores and headed evils
That thou with licence of free foot hast caught
Wouldst thou disgorge into the general world.
   Jaques
70 Why, who cries out on pride
That can therein tax any private party?
Doth it not flow as hugely as the sea
Till that the weary very means do ebb?
What woman in the city do I name
75 When that I say the city-woman bears
The cost of princes on unworthy shoulders?
Who can come in and say that I mean her,
When such a one as she, such is her neighbour?
Or what is he of basest function
80 That says his bravery is not on my cost,
Thinking that I mean him, but therein suits
His folly to the mettle of my speech?
There then! How then? What then? Let me see wherein
My tongue hath wrong'd him. If it do him right,
85 Then he hath wrong'd himself; if he be free,
Why then my taxing like a wild goose flies
Unclaim'd of any man. But who come here?

   Enter Orlando *with sword drawn*

   Orlando
Forbear, and eat no more!
   Jaques
Why, I have eat none yet.
   Orlando
90 Nor shalt not, till necessity be serv'd.
   Jaques
Of what kind should this cock come of?
   Duke Senior
Art thou thus bolden'd, man, by thy distress,

94 *civility*: civilized behaviour.

95 *my vein*: condition, state of mind.

97 *am I . . . bred*: I was brought up in civilized society.
98 *nurture*: education.

100 *answered*: answerèd; provided for.

101 *And . . . die*: Jaques may start eating here—or perhaps offer some grapes (making a pun on 'reason'/'raisin'). *answered*: answerèd.
102 *gentleness*: good breeding. *force*: prevail.

106 *gently*: politely.
107 *had been*: would have been.

109 *commandment*: authority.
110 *desert*: lonely place.
111 *melancholy*: dismal.
112 *Lose*: forget.

114 *knoll'd*: rung.
115 *goodman*: host.

118 *gentleness*: courtesy.
119 *hide*: sheathe.

125 *upon command*: as you wish.
126 *wanting*: need.

Or else a rude despiser of good manners
That in civility thou seem'st so empty?
   Orlando
95 You touch'd my vein at first: the thorny point
Of bare distress hath ta'en from me the show
Of smooth civility; yet am I inland bred
And know some nurture. But forbear, I say;
He dies that touches any of this fruit
100 Till I and my affairs are answered.
   Jaques
And you will not be answered with reason, I must die.
   Duke Senior
What would you have? Your gentleness shall force
More than your force move us to gentleness.
   Orlando
I almost die for food, and let me have it.
   Duke Senior
105 Sit down and feed, and welcome to our table.
   Orlando
Speak you so gently? Pardon me, I pray you:
I thought that all things had been savage here
And therefore put I on the countenance
Of stern commandment. But whate'er you are
110 That in this desert inaccessible,
Under the shade of melancholy boughs,
Lose and neglect the creeping hours of time—
If ever you have look'd on better days,
If ever been where bells have knoll'd to church,
115 If ever sat at any goodman's feast,
If ever from your eyelids wip'd a tear,
And know what 'tis to pity and be pitied,
Let gentleness my strong enforcement be,
In the which hope, I blush, and hide my sword.
   Duke Senior
120 True is it that we have seen better days,
And have with holy bell been knoll'd to church,
And sat at goodmen's feasts, and wip'd our eyes
Of drops that sacred pity hath engender'd:
And therefore sit you down in gentleness
125 And take upon command what help we have
That to your wanting may be minister'd.

'All the world's a stage' (*2*, 7, 139) Alan Rickman as Jaques, Royal Shakespeare Company, 1985.

127 *forebear*: abstain from.

Orlando
Then but forbear your food a little while
Whiles, like a doe, I go to find my fawn
And give it food: there is an old poor man
130 Who after me hath many a weary step

131 *suffic'd*: satisfied.
132 *weak*: causing weakness.
133 *bit*: bite, mouthful.

Limp'd in pure love. Till he be first suffic'd,
Oppress'd with two weak evils, age and hunger,
I will not touch a bit.
Duke Senior
                                      Go find him out.
And we will nothing waste till you return.
Orlando

134 *waste*: consume.
135 *be blest*: may you be blessed.
136 *all . . . unhappy*: the only unfortunate people.
140 *all . . . players*: Jaques seems to allude to the motto of the new Globe theatre: *Totus mundus agit histrionem* (all the world plays the actor).

135 I thank ye, and be blest for your good comfort. [*Exit*
Duke Senior
Thou see'st we are not all alone unhappy:
This wide and universal theatre
Presents more woeful pageants than the scene
Wherein we play in.
Jaques
                          All the world's a stage

140 And all the men and women merely players:
They have their exits and their entrances
And one man in his time plays many parts,
His acts being seven ages. At first the infant,
Mewling and puking in the nurse's arms;

144 *Mewling and puking*: whimpering and vomiting (the earliest recorded uses of these words).
149 *Made to*: on the subject of.
150 *strange*: foreign.
bearded . . . pard: with facial hair like a leopard's whiskers.
151 *Jealous*: suspiciously careful.
sudden: impetuous.
152 *bubble*: 'Honour (reputation) is a bubble' (proverbial).
153 *justice*: judge, magistrate.
154 *capon*: chicken (a castrated cock bred for the table, often used to bribe a judge).
156 *saws*: sayings, proverbs.
modern instances: commonplace examples.
158 *pantaloon*: Pantalone, the ridiculous old merchant of the *commedia dell'arte*.
159 *pouch*: purse.

145 Then the whining schoolboy with his satchel
And shining morning face, creeping like snail
Unwillingly to school; and then the lover,
Sighing like furnace, with a woeful ballad
Made to his mistress' eyebrow; then a soldier,
150 Full of strange oaths and bearded like the pard,
Jealous in honour, sudden, and quick in quarrel,
Seeking the bubble 'reputation'
Even in the cannon's mouth; and then the justice,
In fair round belly with good capon lin'd,
155 With eyes severe and beard of formal cut,
Full of wise saws and modern instances—
And so he plays his part; the sixth age shifts
Into the lean and slipper'd pantaloon,
With spectacles on nose and pouch on side,

160 His youthful hose well sav'd—a world too wide
For his shrunk shank—and his big manly voice,
Turning again toward childish treble, pipes
And whistles in his sound; last scene of all
That ends this strange eventful history
165 Is second childishness and mere oblivion,
Sans teeth, sans eyes, sans taste, sans everything.

Enter Orlando *with* Adam *on his back*

Duke Senior
Welcome. Set down your venerable burden,
And let him feed.
Orlando
               I thank you most for him.
Adam
So had you need: I scarce can speak
170 To thank you for myself.
Duke Senior
Welcome; fall to: I will not trouble you
As yet to question you about your fortunes.—
Give us some music, and, good cousin, sing.

Song

Amiens
   Blow, blow, thou winter wind,
175   Thou art not so unkind
   As man's ingratitude;
   Thy tooth is not so keen,
   Because thou art not seen,
   Although thy breath be rude.
180   He-ho, sing hey-ho
        Unto the green holly,
        Most friendship is feigning,
        Most loving mere folly.
        The hey-ho, the holly,
185   This life is most jolly.

160 *His . . . hose*: the breeches he wore
    when he was young.
    a world: far.
161 *shank*: calf, leg.
163 *his*: its.
164 *eventful*: The first recorded use of this
    word.
    history: history play.
165 *mere oblivion*: complete forgetfulness.
166 *Sans*: without.
168 *most for him*: especially on his behalf.
171 *fall to*: start eating.
172 *to question*: by questioning (although
    he must be doing this during the
    song).
173 *cousin*: A friendly address from a
    prince to a lord.
175 *unkind*: unnatural, harsh.

179 *rude*: cruel.

181 *holly*: The tree was associated from
    Roman times with winter and good
    (male) friendship.
182 *feigning*: pretence.

187 *nigh*: deeply.

188 *benefits forgot*: forgotten favours.

189 *warp*: shrink, turn to ice.

> Freeze, freeze, thou bitter sky,
> That dost not bite so nigh
> As benefits forgot;
> Though thou the waters warp,
190   Thy sting is not so sharp
> As friend remember'd not.
>   He-ho, sing hey-ho
>   Unto the green holly,
>   Most friendship is feigning,
195   Most loving mere folly.
>   The hey-ho, the holly,
>   This life is most jolly.

Duke Senior

If that you were the good Sir Roland's son,
As you have whisper'd faithfully you were,

200 *effigies*: likeness; the word is stressed on the second syllable.

201 *limn'd*: depicted.

200 And as mine eye doth his effigies witness
Most truly limn'd and living in your face,
Be truly welcome hither. I am the duke

203 *residue . . . fortunes*: remainder of your story.

That lov'd your father. The residue of your fortune
Go to my cave and tell me.—Good old man,

205 *right*: very.

205 Thou art right welcome as thy master is.—
[*To* Orlando] Support him by the arm. [*To* Adam]
   Give me your hand,
And let me all your fortunes understand.   [*Exeunt*

'Hang there, my verse, in witness of my love' (3, 2, 1). Liam Cunningham as Orlando, Royal Shakespeare Company, 1996.

ACT 3

Act 3 Scene 1
Duke Frederick threatens Oliver.

SCENE 1

Enter Duke Frederick, Lords, *and* Oliver

Duke Frederick
'Not see him since'? Sir, sir, that cannot be!
But were I not the better part made mercy,
I should not seek an absent argument
Of my revenge, thou present. But look to it:
5 Find out thy brother, wheresoe'er he is;
Seek him with candle; bring him dead or living
Within this twelvemonth, or turn thou no more
To seek a living in our territory.
Thy lands and all things that thou dost call thine
10 Worth seizure, do we seize into our hands
Till thou canst quit thee by thy brother's mouth
Of what we think against thee.
Oliver
O that your highness knew my heart in this:
I never lov'd my brother in my life.
Duke Frederick
15 More villain thou. [*To* Lords] Well, push him out of
    doors
And let my officers of such a nature
Make an extent upon his house and lands.
Do this expediently and turn him going.
                                    [*Exeunt severally*

SCENE 2

Enter Orlando *with a paper*

Orlando
Hang there, my verse, in witness of my love;
And thou, thrice-crowned queen of night, survey
With thy chaste eye, from thy pale sphere above,

Act 3 Scene 1
Duke Frederick threatens Oliver.

2 *were . . . mercy*: if I were not for the
most part made of mercy.
3–4 *seek . . . present*: try to get my
revenge on someone who is absent,
when you are here.
3 *argument*: subject.
6 *with candle*: diligently (perhaps
alluding to the parable of the woman
who, 'if she lose one piece [of silver]
doth . . . light a candle . . . and seek
diligently till she find it' (Luke 15:8)).
7 *turn*: return.
10 *seizure*: legal confiscation.
11 *quit thee*: acquit yourself.
mouth: testimony.

15 *More . . . thou*: Duke Frederick
(ironically) condemns himself.
16 *of . . . nature*: experienced in such
things.
17 *Make . . . upon*: draw up a writ and
seize.
18 *expediently*: expeditiously, quickly.
turn . . . going: send him on his way.

Act 3 Scene 2
In a short moonlit interlude, Orlando hangs
his poem on a tree.

1 *witness*: testimony.
2 *thrice . . . night*: The moon goddess
ruled as Cynthia in the heavens, Diana
on earth, and Proserpina in the
underworld.
crowned: crownèd.

4 *Thy huntress' name*: Orlando imagines
   Rosalind as one of the followers of
   Diana (who was also goddess of
   chastity).
   full: entire.
   sway: control.
6 *character*: inscribe.
8 *witness'd*: attested.
10 *unexpressive*: inexpressible,
   indescribable.
   she: woman.
10s.d. *Exit*: Orlando's departure leaves
   the stage empty, so marking the end
   of a scene.

Act 3 Scene 3
A debate on town life versus country life.
Rosalind and Celia read Orlando's verses,
and Rosalind (disguised as Ganymede)
offers to cure Orlando of his love.

3 *in respect of*: with regard to.

4 *in respect that*: considering.
   naught: worthless, useless.
5 *solitary*: alone, not in company.
6 *private*: lonely.

8 *spare*: frugal.

9 *humour*: disposition.

10 *stomach*: a) appetite; b) inclination.
   philosophy: practical wisdom.

13 *wants*: lacks.

14 *means*: resources.
   content: happiness.

17 *wit*: knowledge.

18 *nature nor art*: birth or education.
18–19 *complain . . . kindred*: Corin's
   reversal of these is perhaps satirical.
18 *breeding*: upbringing.
19 *dull kindred*: stupid family.
20 *natural philosopher*: a) student of
   science; b) fool.

Thy huntress' name that my full life doth sway.
5 O Rosalind, these trees shall be my books,
   And in their barks my thoughts I'll character
   That every eye which in this forest looks
   Shall see thy virtue witness'd everywhere.
   Run, run, Orlando, carve on every tree
10 The fair, the chaste, and unexpressive she.   [*Exit*

SCENE 3

The forest: enter Corin *and* Touchstone

Corin
And how like you this shepherd's life, Master
Touchstone?
Touchstone
Truly, shepherd, in respect of itself, it is a good life; but
in respect that it is a shepherd's life, it is naught. In
5 respect that it is solitary, I like it very well; but in respect
that it is private, it is a very vile life. Now in respect it is
in the fields, it pleaseth me well; but in respect it is not
in the court, it is tedious. As it is a spare life, look you, it
fits my humour well; but as there is no more plenty in it,
10 it goes much against my stomach. Hast any philosophy
in thee, shepherd?
Corin
No more but that I know the more one sickens, the
worse at ease he is; and that he that wants money,
means, and content is without three good friends; that
15 the property of rain is to wet and fire to burn; that good
pasture makes fat sheep; and that a great cause of the
night is lack of the sun; that he that hath learned no wit
by nature nor art may complain of good breeding, or
comes of a very dull kindred.
Touchstone
20 Such a one is a natural philosopher.—Wast ever in
court, shepherd?

Corin

No, truly.

Touchstone

Then thou art damned.

Corin

24 *I hope*: I hope not.

Nay, I hope.

Touchstone

25-6 *ill-roasted . . . side*: Eggs, roasted in hot ashes, were spoiled if not turned.

25 Truly thou art damned: like an ill-roasted egg, all on one side.

Corin

For not being at court? Your reason.

Touchstone

28 *good*: a) courtly; b) morally correct.

29-30 *thy manners*: a) your morals; b) your behaviour.

31 *parlous*: perilous.

Why, if thou never wast at court, thou never saw'st good manners; if thou never saw'st good manners, then thy

30 manners must be wicked, and wickedness is sin, and sin is damnation. Thou art in a parlous state, shepherd.

Corin

32 *Not a whit*: not in the least.

Not a whit, Touchstone: those that are good manners at the court are as ridiculous in the country as the behaviour of the country is most mockable at the court.

35 *salute not*: do not greet one another. *but you kiss*: without kissing.

35 You told me you salute not at the court but you kiss your hands: that courtesy would be uncleanly if courtiers were shepherds.

Touchstone

38 *Instance*: give me proof of that.

Instance, briefly; come, instance.

Corin

39 *still*: always. *fells*: fleeces.

Why, we are still handling our ewes, and their fells, you

40 know, are greasy.

Touchstone

41 *your*: those.

43 *Shallow*: too easy.

Why, do not your courtier's hands sweat, and is not the grease of a mutton as wholesome as the sweat of a man? Shallow, shallow! A better instance, I say—come.

Corin

Besides, our hands are hard.

Touchstone

45 Your lips will feel them the sooner. Shallow again: a more sounder instance, come.

Corin

47 *tarred over*: covered in tar (used to stop bleeding from shearing cuts).

49 *civet*: perfume (which was based on a secretion from the anal glands of the civet cat).

And they are often tarred over with the surgery of our sheep, and would you have us kiss tar? The courtiers' hands are perfumed with civet.

50 *worms' meat*: food for worms.
   respect of: comparison with.
51 *good . . . flesh*: fine human being.
52 *perpend*: ponder, think about it.
53 *flux*: discharge.
   Mend the instance: improve your
   argument.
54 *rest*: cease.

56 *God . . . thee*: i.e. in order to let blood
   (a possible cure for madness).
   raw: naive, immature.
57 *true*: trustworthy.
   get: earn.

59 *content . . . harm*: am resigned to my
   affliction.

62 *simple*: a) foolish; b) unashamed.

63 *offer*: presume.

64 *cattle*: beasts.
   bawd: pander, pimp.
   bell-wether: leading sheep of a flock
   (which followed the leader's bell).
65 *crooked-pated*: with crooked horns
   (symbolic of a cuckold).
66 *cuckoldly*: possessed of an unfaithful
   wife.
   match: manner.
67–8 *the devil . . . shepherds*: it's
   because even the devil refuses to
   admit shepherds to hell.
68 *else*: otherwise.
   'scape: escape.

71 *'From . . . Inde*: from the East Indies
   (India and the islands of the Malay
   archipelago) to the West Indies (both
   associated with wealth and gems);
   'Inde' was pronounced to rhyme with
   'mind'.
73 *worth*: merit.

75 *lin'd*: sketched.
76 *black*: foul, ugly.
   to: compared with.

78 *fair*: beauty.

Touchstone

50 Most shallow man! Thou worms' meat in respect of a
good piece of flesh, indeed! Learn of the wise and
perpend: civet is of a baser birth than tar, the very
uncleanly flux of a cat. Mend the instance, shepherd.

Corin

You have too courtly a wit for me; I'll rest.

Touchstone

55 Wilt thou rest damned? God help thee, shallow man.
God make incision in thee, thou art raw.

Corin

Sir, I am a true labourer: I earn that I eat, get that I wear,
owe no man hate, envy no man's happiness, glad of
other men's good, content with my harm; and the
60 greatest of my pride is to see my ewes graze and my
lambs suck.

Touchstone

That is another simple sin in you: to bring the ewes and
the rams together and to offer to get your living by the
copulation of cattle; to be bawd to a bell-wether and to
65 betray a she-lamb of a twelvemonth to a crooked-pated
old cuckoldly ram out of all reasonable match. If thou
be'st not damned for this, the devil himself will have no
shepherds. I cannot see else how thou shouldst 'scape.

Corin

Here comes young Monsieur Ganymede, my new
70 mistress's brother.

Enter Rosalind *as* Ganymede

Rosalind

[*Reading from a paper*]
   'From the East to Western Inde
     No jewel is like Rosalind;
   Her worth, being mounted on the wind,
     Through all the world bears Rosalind;
75   All the pictures fairest lin'd
     Are but black to Rosalind;
   Let no face be kept in mind
     But the fair of Rosalind.'

80–1 *the right . . . market*: just like the jog-trot rhythm of dairy-women riding to market.

82 *Out*: be quiet.

84 *hart*: male deer.
hind: female deer.

86 *kind*: mate.

88 *Winter'd*: adapted for winter.

90 *sheaf*: gather into sheaves.
91 *to cart*: a) to carry away; b) to be whipped behind a cart (the punishment for a prostitute).

94 *find*: suffer.

96 *false gallop*: canter (proverbial description of unmetrical verse).

100 *graft*: engraft (by inserting a shoot from another tree).
101 *medlar*: a) species of apple eaten only when over-ripe; b) interfering person ('meddler').
102–3 *right virtue*: true quality.

Touchstone
I'll rhyme you so eight years together, dinners and
80 suppers and sleeping-hours excepted. It is the right
butter-women's rank to market.
Rosalind
Out, fool!
Touchstone
For a taste:
  If a hart do lack a hind,
85   Let him seek out Rosalind;
  If the cat will after kind,
    So be sure will Rosalind;
  Winter'd garments must be lin'd,
    So must slender Rosalind;
90   They that reap must sheaf and bind,
    Then to cart with Rosalind;
  Sweetest nut hath sourest rind,
    Such a nut is Rosalind;
  He that sweetest rose will find,
95   Must find love's prick—and Rosalind.
This is the very false gallop of verses: why do you infect
yourself with them?
Rosalind
Peace, you dull fool. I found them on a tree.
Touchstone
Truly, the tree yields bad fruit.
Rosalind
100 I'll graft it with you, and then I shall graft it with a
medlar; then it will be the earliest fruit i'th'country, for
you'll be rotten ere you be half ripe, and that's the right
virtue of the medlar.
Touchstone
You have said—but whether wisely or no, let the forest
105 judge.

Enter Celia *as* Aliena *with a writing*

Rosalind
Peace, here comes my sister, reading. Stand aside.

107 *desert*: uninhabited place.

108 *For*: because.

110 *civil*: civilized, sophisticated.

112 *erring*: a) wandering; b) sinful.

113 *stretching . . . span*: fully extended hand.

114 *Buckles in*: encompasses.
    sum of age: whole lifetime.

118 *sentence*: witty saying.

121 *quintessence*: purest form; the 'fifth essence' was thought to be a distillation of the other four 'essences' or elements of the terrestrial world.
    sprite: spirit.

122 *in little*: in miniature.

123 *Heaven . . . charg'd*: Heaven ordered Nature.

125 *wide-enlarg'd*: spread widely (through all women).

126 *presently*: immediately.

127 *Helen's . . . heart*: the beauty but not the falseness of Helen of Troy.

128 *Cleopatra*: the Queen of Egypt.

129 *Atalanta's . . . part*: Atalanta preserved her chastity by insisting that suitors should be able to outrun her.

130 *Lucretia*: Lucrece killed herself when she had been raped by Tarquin.

131 *of*: from.

132 *heavenly synod*: a council of divinities.

134 *touches*: features.

135 *would*: willed.

136 *And I to*: and that I should.

137 *Jupiter*: the god whom Rosalind invoked earlier (*2, 4, 1*).

138 *homily*: moral lecture.

140 *Backfriends*: false friends, traitors (for apparently spying on her).

141 *sirrah*: A dismissive, even contemptuous, form of address.

Celia

'Why should this a desert be?
  For it is unpeopled? No:
Tongues I'll hang on every tree,
  That shall civil sayings show: 110
Some how brief the life of man
  Runs his erring pilgrimage
That the stretching of a span
  Buckles in his sum of age; 115
Some of violated vows
  'Twixt the souls of friend and friend;
But upon the fairest boughs
  Or at every sentence end
Will I "Rosalinda" write, 120
  Teaching all that read to know
The quintessence of every sprite
  Heaven would in little show.
Therefore Heaven Nature charg'd
  That one body should be fill'd 125
With all graces wide-enlarg'd;
  Nature presently distill'd
Helen's cheek but not her heart,
  Cleopatra's majesty,
Atalanta's better part, 130
  Sad Lucretia's modesty.
Thus Rosalind of many parts
  By heavenly synod was devis'd,
Of many faces, eyes, and hearts,
  To have the touches dearest priz'd. 135
Heaven would that she these gifts should have,
  And I to live and die her slave.'

Rosalind

[*Coming forward*] O most gentle Jupiter, what tedious homily of love have you wearied your parishioners withal, and never cried, 'Have patience, good people!'

Celia

How now? Backfriends!—Shepherd, go off a little.—Go 140 with him, sirrah.

Touchstone

Come, shepherd, let us make an honourable retreat,

143 *bag and baggage*: all the (military)
  equipment; Touchstone probably puns
  on 'baggage' = slut, strumpet.
143–4 *scrip and scrippage*: wallet and its
  contents (Touchstone's coinage).
145 *verses*: lines of poetry.

147, 148 *feet*: a) metrical feet; b) feet of
  the body.

148 *bear*: tolerate.

149 *bear*: carry.
150 *without*: outside.

154 *I . . . wonder*: I had already
  experienced most of it; Rosalind
  alludes to the proverbial phrase 'a
  nine days' wonder' (= a short-lived
  phenomenon).
155 *palm-tree*: willow tree.
156 *so berhymed*: written about in rhymes.
  Pythagoras: The Greek philosopher
  taught that souls migrated from
  humans to beasts.
157 *Irish rat*: It was a popular joke that the
  Irish rid themselves of rats (and other
  enemies) by incantation.
158 *Trow you*: can you tell.
160–1 *Change you colour*: are you
  blushing.

163–5 *it is . . . encounter*: Celia inverts the
  proverb, 'Friends may meet, but
  mountains never greet'.
164 *with*: by means of.

168 *petitionary vehemence*: passionate
  pleading.

though not with bag and baggage, yet with scrip and
scrippage.   [*Exeunt* Touchstone *and* Corin
   Celia
145 Didst thou hear these verses?
   Rosalind
O yes, I heard them all, and more too, for some of them
had in them more feet than the verses would bear.
   Celia
That's no matter: the feet might bear the verses.
   Rosalind
Aye, but the feet were lame and could not bear
150 themselves without the verse, and therefore stood
lamely in the verse.
   Celia
But didst thou hear without wondering how thy name
should be hanged and carved upon these trees?
   Rosalind
I was seven of the nine days out of the wonder before
155 you came, for look here what I found on a palm-tree. I
was never so berhymed since Pythagoras' time that I
was an Irish rat—which I can hardly remember.
   Celia
Trow you who hath done this?
   Rosalind
Is it a man?
   Celia
160 And a chain that you once wore about his neck? Change
you colour?
   Rosalind
I prithee, who?
   Celia
O Lord, Lord, it is a hard matter for friends to meet, but
mountains may be removed with earthquakes and so
165 encounter.
   Rosalind
Nay, but who is it?
   Celia
Is it possible?
   Rosalind
Nay, I prithee now, with most petitionary vehemence,
tell me who it is.

171–2 *out . . . hooping*: beyond all
        exclamation.

173 *Good my complexion*: spare my
        blushes.
174 *caparisoned*: dressed up.
174–5 *I have . . . disposition*: my nature
        wears a man's attire.
175–6 *One . . . discovery*: any more delay
        seems as long as a voyage of
        exploration to the South Pacific
        Ocean.
175 *prithee*: pray you.
177 *apace*: fast.

182 *So*: thus.
183 *of God's making*: The expression (= a
        normal human being) was proverbial.
187 *stay*: wait for.

191–2 *sad . . . maid*: seriously and
        honestly.

198 *Wherein . . . he*: what was he wearing.
        makes: does.

Celia

170 O wonderful, wonderful, and most wonderful
wonderful, and yet again wonderful, and after that out
of all hooping.

Rosalind

Good my complexion, dost thou think, though I am
caparisoned like a man, I have a doublet and hose in my
175 disposition? One inch of delay more is a South Sea of
discovery. I prithee tell me who is it—quickly, and speak
apace. I would thou couldst stammer that thou might'st
pour this concealed man out of thy mouth as wine
comes out of a narrow-mouthed bottle: either too
180 much at once or none at all. I prithee take the cork out
of thy mouth that I may drink thy tidings.

Celia

So you may put a man in your belly.

Rosalind

Is he of God's making? What manner of man? Is his
head worth a hat or his chin worth a beard?

Celia

185 Nay, he hath but a little beard.

Rosalind

Why, God will send more if the man will be thankful.
Let me stay the growth of his beard, if thou delay me not
the knowledge of his chin.

Celia

It is young Orlando, that tripped up the wrestler's heels
190 and your heart both in an instant.

Rosalind

Nay, but the devil take mocking! Speak sad brow and
true maid.

Celia

I'faith, coz, 'tis he.

Rosalind

Orlando?

Celia

195 Orlando.

Rosalind

Alas the day, what shall I do with my doublet and hose?
What did he when thou saw'st him? What said he? How
looked he? Wherein went he? What makes he here? Did

199 *remains*: dwells.

202 *Gargantua*: a giant with a phenomenal appetite, created by the French writer Rabelais.
204 *particulars*: questions.
205 *a catechism*: a method of instruction using simple questions and answers.

207 *freshly*: healthy.

209 *atomies*: specks of dust.
resolve: answer.
210 *propositions*: questions, problems.
210–11 *take . . . observance*: try hearing how I found him, and enjoy [my story] by paying attention.

213 *Jove's tree*: The oak tree was sacred to Jupiter.

215 *audience*: hearing.

218 *becomes*: adorns.

220 *'holla'*: whoa, stop (as to a horse).
curvets: prances along.
221 *unseasonably*: in an ill-timed manner.
furnished: dressed, equipped.
222 *heart*: A pun on heart/hart.

223 *would*: should like to.
burden: continuous undersong, interruption.
bring'st: put.

he ask for me? Where remains he? How parted he with
200 thee? And when shalt thou see him again? Answer me in
one word.
Celia
You must borrow me Gargantua's mouth first: 'tis a
word too great for any mouth of this age's size. To say
'aye' and 'no' to these particulars is more than to answer
205 in a catechism.
Rosalind
But doth he know that I am in this forest and in man's
apparel? Looks he as freshly as he did the day he
wrestled?
Celia
It is as easy to count atomies as to resolve the
210 propositions of a lover; but take a taste of my finding
him and relish it with good observance. I found him
under a tree like a dropped acorn.
Rosalind
[*Aside*] It may well be called Jove's tree when it drops
forth such fruit.
Celia
215 Give me audience, good madam.
Rosalind
Proceed.
Celia
There lay he stretched along like a wounded knight.
Rosalind
Though it be pity to see such a sight, it well becomes the
ground.
Celia
220 Cry 'holla' to thy tongue, I prithee: it curvets
unseasonably. He was furnished like a hunter.
Rosalind
O ominous: he comes to kill my heart.
Celia
I would sing my song without a burden; thou bring'st
me out of tune.
Rosalind
225 Do you not know I am a woman? When I think, I must
speak. Sweet, say on.

Enter Orlando *and* Jaques

Celia

You bring me out.—Soft, comes he not here?

Rosalind

'Tis he. Slink by, and note him.

Rosalind and Celia stand aside

Jaques

227 *bring me out*: make me forget my words.

I thank you for your company, but, good faith, I had as
230 lief have been myself alone.

229-30 *had as lief*: would rather.

Orlando

And so had I. But yet, for fashion sake, I thank you too
for your society.

232 *society*: company.

Jaques

God buy you. Let's meet as little as we can.

233 *God buy you*: goodbye (from 'God be with you').

Orlando

I do desire we may be better strangers.

234 *better strangers*: more distant from each other.

Jaques

235 I pray you mar no more trees with writing love-songs in
their barks.

Orlando

I pray you mar no mo of my verses with reading them
ill-favouredly.

237 *mo*: more.
238 *ill-favouredly*: badly.

Jaques

'Rosalind' is your love's name?

Orlando

240 Yes, just.

240 *just*: exactly.

Jaques

I do not like her name.

Orlando

There was no thought of pleasing you when she was
christened.

Jaques

What stature is she of?

Orlando

245 Just as high as my heart.

246 *pretty*: clever.
246-8 *have . . . rings*: Jaques suggests that Orlando has learned ('conned') his rhymes from the inscriptions in rings.

Jaques

You are full of pretty answers: have you not been
acquainted with goldsmiths' wives and conned them
out of rings?

249–50 *I answer . . . questions*: Orlando accuses Jaques of taking his remarks from the painted wall-hangings (with balloons for spoken words) used in taverns and private houses.

251–2 *Atalanta's heels*: See above, line 129 note.
252–3 *rail against*: complain about.
254 *breather*: living creature.
259 *troth*: faith.
   fool: i.e. Touchstone.
262 *figure*: likeness.
263 *cipher*: the figure '0', nothing.

264 *tarry*: delay, linger.

268 *saucy lackey*: cheeky footman.
268–9 *under that habit*: in that disguise.
269 *play the knave*: a) act like a boy;
   b) trick and defeat him (as in a game of cards).

271 *What would you*: what do you want.

Orlando

Not so; but I answer you right painted cloth, from
250 whence you have studied your questions.

Jaques

You have a nimble wit; I think 'twas made of Atalanta's
heels. Will you sit down with me, and we two will rail
against our mistress the world and all our misery.

Orlando

I will chide no breather in the world but myself, against
255 whom I know most faults.

Jaques

The worst fault you have is to be in love.

Orlando

'Tis a fault I will not change for your best virtue: I am
weary of you.

Jaques

By my troth, I was seeking for a fool, when I found you.

Orlando

260 He is drowned in the brook: look but in, and you shall
see him.

Jaques

There I shall see mine own figure.

Orlando

Which I take to be either a fool or a cipher.

Jaques

I'll tarry no longer with you. Farewell, good Signor
265 Love.

Orlando

I am glad of your departure. Adieu, good Monsieur
Melancholy.   [*Exit* Jaques

Rosalind

I will speak to him like a saucy lackey, and under that
habit play the knave with him. [*To* Orlando] Do you
270 hear, forester?

Orlando

Very well. What would you?

Rosalind

I pray you, what is't o'clock?

Orlando

You should ask me what time o'day: there's no clock in
the forest.

Rosalind

275 Then there is no true lover in the forest, else sighing
every minute and groaning every hour would detect the
lazy foot of Time as well as a clock.

Orlando

And why not the swift foot of Time? Had not that been
as proper?

Rosalind

280 By no means, sir. Time travels in diverse paces with
diverse persons. I'll tell you who Time ambles withal,
who Time trots withal, who Time gallops withal, and
who he stands still withal.

Orlando

I prithee, who doth he trot withal?

Rosalind

285 Marry, he trots hard with a young maid between the
contract of her marriage and the day it is solemnized. If
the interim be but a sennight, Time's pace is so hard
that it seems the length of seven year.

Orlando

Who ambles Time withal?

Rosalind

290 With a priest that lacks Latin, and a rich man that hath
not the gout; for the one sleeps easily because he cannot
study, and the other lives merrily because he feels no
pain; the one lacking the burden of lean and wasteful
learning, the other knowing no burden of heavy tedious

295 penury. These Time ambles withal.

Orlando

Who doth he gallop withal?

Rosalind

With a thief to the gallows; for though he go as softly as
foot can fall, he thinks himself too soon there.

Orlando

Who stays it still withal?

Rosalind

300 With lawyers in the vacation; for they sleep between
term and term, and then they perceive not how Time
moves.

Orlando

Where dwell you, pretty youth?

276 *detect*: reveal.

279 *proper*: appropriate; Time is usually
depicted as wing-footed.

280 *diverse*: different.

281 *ambles withal*: dawdles along with.

285 *hard*: violently.

286 *the contract . . . marriage*: her
betrothal (a formal and binding
engagement).
solemnized: consecrated and made
legally official by the church
ceremony.

287 *interim*: period between.
sennight: week (seven nights).

290 *lacks*: is ignorant of.

293–4 *lean . . . learning*: unrewarding
study that makes him waste away.

294 *tedious*: painful.

297 *softly*: leisurely.

299 *stays*: stands.

300 *vacation*: period during which the
London law-courts are not sitting.

301 *term*: period of court session.

304 *skirts*: border, edge.

306 *Are . . . place*: were you born here.

307 *cony*: rabbit.
   kindled: born.
308 *purchase*: acquire.
309 *removed*: remote.
310 *of*: by.
   religious: Perhaps 'monastic', or
   'scrupulous about matters of speech'.
312 *inland man*: city-dweller.
   courtship: a) courtly life; b) wooing.
313–14 *read . . . lectures*: deliver many
   warning speeches.
315 *touched with*: infected by.
   giddy: frivolous.
316 *generally*: collectively.
   taxed: accused.
320 *halfpence*: Halfpence coined in
   Elizabeth's reign had identical mint
   markings.

321 *his*: its.
323–4 *I . . . sick*: 'They that be whole need
   not a physician, but they that are sick'
   (Matthew 9:12).
323 *physic*: medicine.
324 *haunts*: frequents.
326 *elegies*: love poems.
   brambles: blackberry bushes.
327 *forsooth*: indeed.
   defying: insulting; 'deifying' (= making
   a god of) is a possible emendation
   here.
328 *fancy-monger*: purveyor of fantasies.
329 *quotidian*: fever recurring every day.
331 *love-shaked*: shaken by love-fever.

Rosalind
With this shepherdess, my sister, here in the skirts of the
305 forest, like fringe upon a petticoat.
   Orlando
Are you native of this place?
   Rosalind
As the cony that you see dwell where she is kindled.
   Orlando
Your accent is something finer than you could purchase
in so removed a dwelling.
   Rosalind
310 I have been told so of many; but indeed an old religious
uncle of mine taught me to speak, who was in his youth
an inland man, one that knew courtship too well, for
ironic there he fell in love. I have heard him read many
lectures against it, and I thank God I am not a woman to
315 be touched with so many giddy offences as he hath
generally taxed their whole sex withal.
   Orlando
Can you remember any of the principal evils that he
laid to the charge of women?
   Rosalind
There were none principal; they were all like one
320 another as halfpence are, every one fault seeming
monstrous till his fellow-fault came to match it.
   Orlando
I prithee recount some of them.
   Rosalind
No. I will not cast away my physic but on those that are
sick. There is a man haunts the forest that abuses our
325 young plants with carving 'Rosalind' on their barks;
hangs odes upon hawthorns and elegies on brambles;
all, forsooth, defying the name of Rosalind. If I could
meet that fancy-monger, I would give him some good
counsel, for he seems to have the quotidian of love upon
330 him.
   Orlando
I am he that is so love-shaked. I pray you tell me your
remedy.

'But are you so much in love as your rhymes speak?' (3, 3, 357). Jemma Redgrave as Rosalind and Robert Hands as Orlando, Greenwich Theatre, 1992.

333 *marks*: symptoms.
334 *cage of rushes*: flimsy prison.

Rosalind

There is none of my uncle's marks upon you. He taught me how to know a man in love, in which cage of rushes
335 I am sure you are not prisoner.

Orlando

What were his marks?

Rosalind

A lean cheek, which you have not; a blue eye and sunken, which you have not; an unquestionable spirit, which you have not; a beard neglected, which you have
340 not—but I pardon you for that, for, simply, your having in beard is a younger brother's revenue. Then your hose should be ungartered, your bonnet unbanded, your sleeve unbuttoned, your shoe untied, and everything about you demonstrating a careless desolation. But you
345 are no such man; you are rather point-device in your accoutrements, as loving yourself than seeming the lover of any other.

337 *a blue eye*: dark circles under the eyes.
338 *unquestionable*: impatient.
340 *simply*: in truth.
your having: what you possess.
341 *revenue*: income.
342 *unbanded*: without a hat-band (of some rich fabric).

love

Orlando

Fair youth, I would I could make thee believe I love.

Rosalind   *irony*

Me believe it? You may as soon make her that you love
350 believe it, which I warrant she is apter to do than to confess she does. That is one of the points in the which women still give the lie to their consciences. But, in good sooth, are you he that hangs the verses on the trees wherein Rosalind is so admired?

Orlando

355 I swear to thee, youth, by the white hand of Rosalind, I am that he, that unfortunate he.

Rosalind

But are you so much in love as your rhymes speak?

Orlando

Neither rhyme nor reason can express how much.

Rosalind

Love is merely a madness and, I tell you, deserves as well
360 a dark-house and a whip as madmen do; and the reason why they are not so punished and cured is that the lunacy is so ordinary that the whippers are in love too. Yet I profess curing it by counsel.

344 *careless desolation*: desperate neglect.
345–6 *point-device . . . accoutrements*: meticulous in your apparel; the French words may hint a note of mockery.
346 *as loving*: rather suggesting that you love.
348 *would*: wish.
350 *apter*: more likely.
352 *still*: always.
give . . . consciences: lie about their real feelings.
353 *sooth*: truth.
359 *merely*: entirely.
360 *a dark-house . . . whip*: The usual Elizabethan therapy for the insane (who were thought to be possessed of the devil).
363 *profess*: am expert in.

love

Orlando
Did you ever cure any so?
Rosalind
365 Yes, one, and in this manner. He was to imagine me his
love, his mistress, and I set him every day to woo me. At
which time would I, being but a moonish youth, grieve,
be effeminate, changeable, longing and liking, proud,
fantastical, apish, shallow, inconstant, full of tears, full
370 of smiles; for every passion something, and for no
passion truly anything, as boys and women are, for the
most part, cattle of this colour; would now like him,
now loathe him; then entertain him, then forswear him;
now weep for him, then spit at him; that I drave my
375 suitor from his mad humour of love to a living humour
of madness, which was to forswear the full stream of the
world and to live in a nook, merely monastic. And thus
I cured him, and this way will I take upon me to wash
your liver as clean as a sound sheep's heart, that there
380 shall not be one spot of love in't.
Orlando
I would not be cured, youth.
Rosalind
I would cure you if you would but call me Rosalind and
come every day to my cot and woo me.
Orlando
Now, by the faith of my love, I will. Tell me where it is.
Rosalind
385 Go with me to it and I'll show it you; and by the way you
shall tell me where in the forest you live. Will you go?
Orlando
Will all my heart, good youth.
Rosalind
Nay, you must call me 'Rosalind'.—Come, sister, will
you go?   [*Exeunt*

367 *moonish*: changeable, fickle.

369 *fantastical*: fanciful, capricious.
apish: affected.
370–1 *for every . . . anything*: showing
something of every emotion but really
feeling nothing.
372 *cattle . . . colour*: creatures of this
kind.
373 *entertain*: converse with.
forswear: refuse.
374 *that*: so that.
drave: drove (an archaic form).
375 *mad humour*: whimsical affectation.
living humour: real affliction.
376 *forswear*: renounce.
377 *in . . . monastic*: in complete religious
seclusion.
379 *liver*: the supposed seat of love and
passion.
381 *would not*: do not wish to be.

383 *cot*: cottage.

385 *by*: along.

Act 3 Scene 4
Touchstone wants to get married in the Forest to Audrey, a simple country girl, but Jaques insists they must have a proper wedding.

1 *apace*: quickly.
2 *the man*: your chosen man.
   yet: still.
3 *simple feature*: honest face.

4 *warrant*: protect.

5–6 *the most . . . Goths*: Touchstone embarks on a torrent of sophisticated wordplay.
   capricious: fantastical; the word derives from the Latin *caper*, a goat (emblem of lustfulness).
6 *honest . . . Goths*: The Roman poet was banished to live with a barbarian tribe, the *Getae*, who could not understand his erotic poetry; 'Goths' is pronounced 'goats'.
7 *ill-inhabited*: badly housed.
7–8 *Jove . . . house*: Jupiter (Jove) and his son Mercury were entertained in their poor cottage by a peasant couple, Philemon and his wife Baucis, who became models of humble hospitality; the story is told by Ovid in his *Metamorphoses*.
10 *seconded with*: supported by.
   forward: precocious.
11 *understanding*: intellect.
11–12 *a great . . . room*: a large bill in a little chamber; Touchstone alludes to the mysterious death of the dramatist Christopher Marlowe, who was said to have been killed in a tavern during a quarrel over the 'reckoning'.
13 *made . . . poetical*: endowed you with the faculties of a poet.
14 *honest*: respectable.
16 *feigning*: a) imaginative; b) deceptive.
17 *given to*: in the habit of writing.
18 *feign*: pretend.

24 *hard-favoured*: ugly.
25 *honey . . . sugar*: i.e. too much of a good thing.

Scene 4

The forest: enter Touchstone, Audrey, *with* Jaques *behind, watching them*

Touchstone
Come apace, good Audrey; I will fetch up your goats, Audrey. And how, Audrey, am I the man yet? Doth my simple feature content you?
Audrey
Your features, Lord warrant us—what features?
Touchstone
5 I am here with thee and thy goats as the most capricious poet honest Ovid was among the Goths.
Jaques
O knowledge ill-inhabited, worse than Jove in a thatched house!
Touchstone
When a man's verses cannot be understood, nor a man's
10 good wit seconded with the forward child, understanding, it strikes a man more dead than a great reckoning in a little room. Truly, I would the gods had made thee poetical.
Audrey
I do not know what 'poetical' is. Is it honest in deed and
15 word? Is it a true thing?
Touchstone
No, truly; for the truest poetry is the most feigning, and lovers are given to poetry; and what they swear in poetry it may be said, as lovers, they do feign.
Audrey
Do you wish then that the gods had made me poetical?
Touchstone
20 I do, truly; for thou swear'st to me thou art honest. Now if thou wert a poet, I might have some hope thou didst feign.
Audrey
Would you not have me honest?
Touchstone
No, truly, unless thou wert hard-favoured: for honesty
25 coupled to beauty is to have honey a sauce to sugar.

26 *A material fool*: a fool with much
  sense.

29 *slut*: slattern.

31 *foul*: plain.
34–5 *Sir . . . Martext*: Probably an
  illiterate priest unable to understand
  Latin; the courtesy title 'Sir' was
  placed before the *surname* of graduate
  clergymen.
37 *couple us*: join us together in
  marriage.
38 *would fain*: would like to.
40 *stagger*: waver, hesitate.
42 *assembly*: congregation.
  horn-beasts: horned creatures (e.g.
  Audrey's goats); Touchstone
  sometimes gestures towards the
  theatre audience, implying that these
  also may wear the horns of cuckolds
  (= men with unfaithful wives).

42 *though*: then.
43 *necessary*: inevitable.
45 *knows . . . them*: doesn't know the full
  extent of his wife's infidelity.
46 *the dowry . . . wife*: the marriage-
  portion (usually money) brought by his
  wife.
47 *alone*: only.
48 *rascal*: inferior deer in herd.
49 *walled*: surrounded by a wall.
52 *defence*: the art of self-defence.
53 *a horn . . . want*: being a cuckold
  more estimable than lacking sexual
  satisfaction.

Jaques
A material fool.
  Audrey
Well, I am not fair, and therefore I pray the gods make
me honest.
  Touchstone
Truly, and to cast away honesty upon a foul slut were to
30 put good meat into an unclean dish.
  Audrey
I am not a slut, though I thank the gods I am foul.
  Touchstone
Well, praised be the gods for thy foulness: sluttishness
may come hereafter. But be it as it may be, I will marry
thee, and to that end I have been with Sir Oliver
35 Martext, the vicar of the next village, who hath
promised to meet me in this place of the forest and to
couple us.
  Jaques
I would fain see this meeting.
  Audrey
Well, the gods give us joy.
  Touchstone
40 Amen. A man may, if he were of a fearful heart, stagger
in this attempt; for here we have no temple but the
wood, no assembly but horn-beasts. But what though?
Courage! As horns are odious, they are necessary. It is
said, 'Many a man knows no end of his goods.' Right:
45 many a man has good horns and knows no end of them.
Well, that is the dowry of his wife, 'tis none of his own
getting. Horns? Even so. Poor men alone? No, no: the
noblest deer hath them as huge as the rascal. Is the
single man therefore blessed? No: as a walled town is
50 more worthier than a village, so is the forehead of a
married man more honourable than the bare brow of a
bachelor. And, by how much defence is better than no
skill, by so much is a horn more precious than to want.

Enter Sir Oliver Martext

55 *dispatch us*: marry us.

57 *give the woman*: The marriage ceremony demanded that someone (usually her father) should give away the bride.
58 *I . . . man*: Touchstone does not want to accept second-hand goods.
61 *What-Ye-Call't*: Touchstone pretends to be reluctant to use the pronunciation 'jakes' (= privy).
62 *God'ild you*: may God reward you.
62–3 *last company*: fellowship when we last met.
63 *Even . . . hand*: just a little ceremony taking place.
65 *be covered*: put on your hat.
66 *Motley*: fool (see *1, 2, 39* note).
67 *bow*: curved wood going under the ox's neck and fitting to yoke.

curb: chain passing under horse's jaw and attaching to bit.
68 *bells*: These were worn to frighten the game birds and to make the falcon easier to find.
so . . . desires: like other animals, man has passions (which must be controlled).
69 *bill*: stroke beak against beak.
wedlock: marriage.
70 *breeding*: a) nobility; b) education.
72 *what marriage is*: a) understand the marriage ceremony; b) instruct you in your marital duties.
73 *wainscot*: wood panelling on walls.
75 *green*: unseasoned.
warp: a) lose shape; b) be unfaithful.
76 *I . . . mind*: I am not inclined to it.
of: by.
77 *like*: likely.

Here comes Sir Oliver.—Sir Oliver Martext, you are well
55 met. Will you dispatch us here under this tree, or shall
we go with you to your chapel?
Martext
Is there none here to give the woman?
Touchstone
I will not take her on gift of any man.
Martext
Truly, she must be given, or the marriage is not lawful.
Jaques
60 [*Coming forward*] Proceed, proceed: I'll give her.
Touchstone
Good-even, good Monsieur What-Ye-Call't. How do
you, sir? You are very well met. God'ild you for your last
company; I am very glad to see you. Even a toy in hand
here, sir.

Jaques removes his hat

65 Nay, pray be covered.
Jaques
Will you be married, Motley?
Touchstone
As the ox hath his bow, sir, the horse his curb, and the
falcon her bells, so man hath his desires, and as pigeons
bill, so wedlock would be nibbling.
Jaques
70 And will you, being a man of your breeding, be married
under a bush like a beggar? Get you to church, and have
a good priest that can tell you what marriage is. This
fellow will but join you together as they join wainscot;
then one of you will prove a shrunk panel and, like
75 green timber, warp, warp.
Touchstone
I am not in the mind; but I were better to be married of
him than of another, for he is not like to marry me well
and, not being well married, it will be a good excuse for
me hereafter to leave my wife.
Jaques
80 Go thou with me and let me counsel thee.

82 *bawdry*: unchastity, sin.

83 *O sweet Oliver*: A popular song where
   a lovesick maiden pleads with her
   hardhearted lover.
84 *brave*: handsome.

87 *Wind away*: get away quickly.

90 *fantastical*: whimsical, capricious.
91 *flout*: mock.
   calling: vocation.

Touchstone
Come, sweet Audrey, we must be married or we must
live in bawdry.—Farewell, good Master Oliver. Not
[*Sings*]
    O sweet Oliver,
     O brave Oliver,
85   Leave me not behind thee;
but [*Sings*]
     Wind away,
     Begone, I say,
    I will not to wedding with thee.
Martext
90 [*Aside*] 'Tis no matter; ne'er a fantastical knave of them
all shall flout me out of my calling.   [*Exeunt*

Act 3 Scene 5
Celia teases Rosalind, and Corin tells them
of Phoebe's unkindness to Silvius.

SCENE 5

The forest: enter Rosalind *as* Ganymede *and* Celia *as*
Aliena

1 *Never*: don't.

2 *prithee*: pray you.
  grace: sense of propriety.
3 *become*: suit.

6 *the dissembling colour*: Judas, who
  betrayed Christ with a kiss (Luke
  22:47), was said to have a red beard.
7 *Something*: somewhat.
7–8 *his . . . children*: his kisses are like
  those of Judas.

10 *your*: that.

Rosalind
Never talk to me; I will weep.
Celia
Do, I prithee; but yet have the grace to consider that
tears do not become a man.
Rosalind
But have I not cause to weep?
Celia
5 As good cause as one would desire: therefore weep.
Rosalind
His very hair is of the dissembling colour.
Celia
Something browner than Judas's: marry, his kisses are
Judas's own children.
Rosalind
I'faith, his hair is of a good colour.
Celia
10 An excellent colour: your chestnut was ever the only
colour.

12–13 *holy bread*: bread used in the Service of Holy Communion.

14 *cast*: discarded.
Diana: goddess of chastity.
14–15 *of . . . sisterhood*: vowed to cold and barren chastity.

21 *pickpurse*: pickpocket.
22 *verity*: honesty, constancy.
concave: hollow.

25 *in*: in love.

26 *downright*: plainly.

28 *tapster*: tavern-keeper.
28–9 *confirmers . . . reckonings*: witnesses to false tavern bills.

31 *question*: conversation.

35 *brave*: fine.
37–9 *quite . . . goose*: Orlando's fine declarations of love miss the point, like a novice ('puny') tilter who makes a notable fool of himself by breaking his lance sideways ('quite traverse') across ('athwart') his opponent's body.
38 *spurs . . . side*: i.e. so that it does not charge in a straight line.
39–40 *all's . . . guides*: everything is great when you're young and foolish.

Rosalind

And his kissing is as full of sanctity as the touch of holy bread.

Celia

He hath bought a pair of cast lips of Diana. A nun of
15 winter's sisterhood kisses not more religiously: the very ice of chastity is in them.

Rosalind

But why did he swear he would come this morning and comes not?

Celia

Nay, certainly, there is no truth in him.

Rosalind

20 Do you think so?

Celia

Yes, I think he is not a pickpurse nor a horse-stealer but, for his verity in love, I do think him as concave as a covered goblet or a worm-eaten nut.

Rosalind

Not true in love?

Celia

25 Yes, when he is in; but I think he is not in.

Rosalind

You have heard him swear downright he was.

Celia

'Was' is not 'is'; besides, the oath of a lover is no stronger than the word of a tapster: they are both the confirmers of false reckonings. He attends here in the forest on the
30 duke your father.

Rosalind

I met the duke yesterday and had much question with him; he asked me of what parentage I was. I told him of as good as he: so he laughed and let me go. But what talk we of fathers when there is such a man as Orlando?

Celia

35 O that's a brave man: he writes brave verses, speaks brave words, swears brave oaths, and breaks them bravely, quite traverse, athwart the heart of his lover as a puny tilter that spurs his horse but on one side, breaks his staff like a noble goose. But all's brave that youth
40 mounts and folly guides.—Who comes here?

Enter Corin

Corin
Mistress and master, you have oft enquir'd
After the shepherd that complain'd of love
Who you saw sitting by me on the turf,
Praising the proud disdainful shepherdess
45 That was his mistress.
Celia
                         Well, and what of him?
Corin
If you will see a pageant truly play'd
Between the pale complexion of true love
And the red glow of scorn and proud disdain,
Go hence a little, and I shall conduct you
50 If you will mark it.
Rosalind
                         O come, let us remove,
The sight of lovers feedeth those in love.
Bring us to this sight and you shall say
I'll prove a busy actor in their play.   [*Exeunt*

42 *of*: against.

46 *pageant*: scene, spectacle.

47 *pale complexion*: The sighs of lovers
    were said to dry up the heart's blood.

50 *mark*: watch.
    remove: depart.

Act 3 Scene 6
Phoebe mocks Silvius and his romantic
love, but falls in love herself when Rosalind
appears (as Ganymede).

5 *Falls*: drops.

6 *But first begs*: without begging.

7 *he*: i.e. the executioner.

8–27 *I . . . hurt*: Phoebe's response
becomes a critique of the conventions
of romantic (Petrarchan) love poetry.
9 *for*: because.
10 *murder . . . eye*: A Petrarchan
commonplace.
11 *sure*: certainly.
13 *gates*: eyelids.
atomies: specks of dust.

15 *with . . . heart*: very seriously.

16 *And if*: if indeed.

17 *counterfeit*: pretend.

19 *Lie . . . say*: don't tell lies by saying.

23 *cicatrice . . . impressure*: mark and
hollow impression.

25 *darted*: shot like arrows.

28 *as . . . near*: may the time come soon.

29 *power of fancy*: ability to attract.

SCENE 6

The forest: enter Silvius *and* Phoebe

Silvius
Sweet Phoebe, do not scorn me, do not, Phoebe.
Say that you love me not, but say not so
In bitterness. The common executioner,
Whose heart th'accustom'd sight of death makes hard,
5 Falls not the axe upon the humbled neck
But first begs pardon. Will you sterner be
Than he that dies and lives by bloody drops?

Enter Rosalind *as* Ganymede, Celia *as* Aliena, *and*
Corin; *they stand aside*

Phoebe
I would not be thy executioner;
I fly thee for I would not injure thee.
10 Thou tell'st me there is murder in mine eye:
'Tis pretty, sure, and very probable
That eyes, that are the frail'st and softest things,
Who shut their coward gates on atomies,
Should be call'd tyrants, butchers, murderers!
15 Now I do frown on thee with all my heart;
And if mine eyes can wound, now let them kill thee.
Now counterfeit to swoon, why, now fall down
Or, if thou canst not, O for shame, for shame,
Lie not to say mine eyes are murderers.
20 Now show the wound mine eye hath made in thee.
Scratch thee but with a pin, and there remains
Some scar of it; lean upon a rush,
The cicatrice and capable impressure
Thy palm some moment keeps. But now mine eyes,
25 Which I have darted at thee, hurt thee not,
Nor I am sure there is no force in eyes
That can do hurt.
Silvius
                    O dear Phoebe,
If ever—as that 'ever' may be near—
You meet in some fresh cheek the power of fancy,

31 *love's . . . arrows*: Cupid, the god of
   love, was traditionally pictured with
   bow and arrows.

35 *Who . . . mother*: who do you think
   you are.
36 *insult*: triumph.
37 *What*: even.
39 *Than . . . bed*: who are not even
   attractive in the darkness; compare
   the proverb, 'When candles be out, all
   cats are grey'.
43 *sale-work*: ready-made goods (not
   specially designed).
   Od's: may God save.
44 *tangle*: ensnare.
47 *bugle*: bead of black glass.
50 *South*: the south wind.
51 *properer*: more handsome.
53 *full . . . children*: i.e. by marrying ugly
   women.
54 *glass*: looking-glass.
55 *out of you*: on account of you.
56 *lineaments*: facial features.

59 *friendly*: as a friend.
60 *you . . . markets*: you're not
   everybody's choice; 'As the market
   goes, wives must sell' (proverbial).
61 *Cry*: beg.
62 *Foul . . . scoffer*: foulness is most foul
   when it consists in being scornful.

30   Then shall you know the wounds invisible
      That love's keen arrows make.
         Phoebe
                                    But till that time
      Come not thou near me; and, when that time comes,
      Afflict me with thy mocks, pity me not,
      As till that time I shall not pity thee.
         Rosalind
35   [*Coming forward*] And why, I pray you? Who might be
           your mother
      That you insult, exult, and all at once
      Over the wretched? What though you have no beauty,
      As, by my faith, I see no more in you
      Than without candle may go dark to bed,
40   Must you be therefore proud and pitiless?
      Why, what means this? Why do you look on me?
      I see no more in you than in the ordinary
      Of Nature's sale-work—Od's my little life,
      I think she means to tangle my eyes too.—
45   No, faith, proud mistress, hope not after it;
      'Tis not your inky brows, your black silk hair,
      Your bugle eyeballs, nor your cheek of cream
      That can entame my spirits to your worship.—
      You, foolish shepherd, wherefore do you follow her
50   Like foggy South, puffing with wind and rain?
      You are a thousand times a properer man
      Than she a woman. 'Tis such fools as you
      That makes the world full of ill-favour'd children.
      'Tis not her glass but you that flatters her,
55   And out of you she sees herself more proper
      Than any of her lineaments can show her.—
      But, mistress, know yourself. Down on your knees,

         Phoebe *kneels to* Rosalind

      And thank heaven, fasting, for a good man's love;
      For I must tell you friendly in your ear,
60   Sell when you can: you are not for all markets.
      Cry the man mercy, love him, take his offer,
      Foul is most foul, being foul to be a scoffer.—
      So take her to thee, shepherd; fare you well.

64 *chide*: scold.
   together: without stopping.

68 *sauce*: pepper, rebuke.

70 *ill will*: bad feeling.

72 *in wine*: when intoxicated.

74 *tuft*: clump.
   here . . . by: nearby.
75 *ply her hard*: persist with her.

78 *abus'd in sight*: deceived by what he
   sees.

80 *Dead shepherd*: Phoebe invokes
   Christopher Marlowe (see *3, 4, 11–12*
   note), author of a popular lyric 'The
   Passionate Shepherd to his Love'.
   saw: maxim, saying.
   might: power.
81 *'Whoever . . . sight'*: A line from
   Marlowe's narrative poem, *Hero and
   Leander* (see *4, 1, 86*).

84 *gentle*: noble.

85 *would*: should.

88 *Were . . . extermin'd*: would both be
   destroyed.

89 *neighbourly*: 'Love thy neighbour as
   thyself' (Leviticus 19:18).

Phoebe
Sweet youth, I pray you chide a year together;
65 I had rather hear you chide than this man woo.
   Rosalind
   He's fallen in love with your foulness—[*To* Silvius] and
   she'll fall in love with my anger. If it be so, as fast as she
   answers thee with frowning looks, I'll sauce her with
   bitter words.—Why look you so upon me?
   Phoebe
70 For no ill will I bear you.
   Rosalind
   I pray you do not fall in love with me
   For I am falser than vows made in wine;
   Besides, I like you not.—[*To* Silvius] If you will know
      my house,
   'Tis at the tuft of olives, here hard by.—
75 Will you go, sister?—Shepherd, ply her hard.—
   Come, sister.—Shepherdess, look on him better
   And be not proud, though all the world could see,
   None could be so abus'd in sight as he.—
   Come, to our flock.   [*Exit with* Celia *and* Corin
   Phoebe
80 Dead shepherd, now I find thy saw of might:
   'Who ever lov'd that lov'd not at first sight?'
   Silvius
   Sweet Phoebe,—
   Phoebe
                     Ha, what say'st thou, Silvius?
   Silvius
   Sweet Phoebe, pity me.
   Phoebe
   Why I am sorry for thee, gentle Silvius.
   Silvius
85 Wherever sorrow is, relief would be.
   If you do sorrow at my grief in love,
   By giving love your sorrow and my grief
   Were both extermin'd.
   Phoebe
   Thou hast my love: is not that neighbourly?
   Silvius
90 I would have you.

90 *were covetousness*: would be greedy: 'Thou shalt not covet thy neighbour's house, thou shalt not covet thy neighbour's wife . . . ' (Exodus 20:17).
91 *the time was*: once upon a time.
92 *yet . . . not*: the time has not yet come.
94 *erst*: formerly.
96 *recompense*: reward.

99 *poverty of grace*: lack of good fortune.
100–2 *That . . . reaps*: that I shall think myself well rewarded if I can take the leftover scraps; Silvius alludes to Leviticus 19:10, in which the owner of the harvest is instructed to leave some corn 'for the poor and stranger'.
101 *glean*: gather.
   broken ears: fallen ears of corn.
102 *Loose*: let fall.
103 *scatter'd*: random.
104 *erewhile*: a little time ago.
106 *bounds*: tracts of land.
107 *carlot*: carl, peasant (the absentee landlord).

109 *peevish*: silly, perverse.

114 *proper*: handsome.
115 *complexion*: appearance.

120 *lusty*: luxurious.

122 *constant . . . damask*: red rose and the pink and white damask rose.
124 *parcels*: separate parts, items.

Phoebe

          Why, that were covetousness.
Silvius, the time was that I hated thee,
And yet it is not that I bear thee love;
But since that thou canst talk of love so well,
Thy company, which erst was irksome to me,
95 I will endure—and I'll employ thee too.
But do not look for further recompense
Than thine own gladness that thou art employ'd.
    Silvius
So holy and so perfect is my love,
And I in such a poverty of grace
100 That I shall think it a most plenteous crop
To glean the broken ears after the man
That the main harvest reaps. Loose now and then
A scatter'd smile, and that I'll live upon.
    Phoebe
Know'st thou the youth that spoke to me erewhile?
    Silvius
105 Not very well; but I have met him oft
And he hath bought the cottage and the bounds
That the old carlot once was master of.
    Phoebe
Think not I love him, though I ask for him;
'Tis but a peevish boy—yet he talks well.
110 But what care I for words? Yet words do well
When he that speaks them pleases those that hear.
It is a pretty youth—not very pretty;
But sure he's proud—and yet his pride becomes him;
He'll make a proper man. The best thing in him
115 Is his complexion; and faster than his tongue
Did make offence, his eye did heal it up;
He is not very tall, yet for his years he's tall;
His leg is but so-so, and yet 'tis well;
There was a pretty redness in his lip,
120 A little riper and more lusty red
Than that mix'd in his cheek; 'twas just the difference
Betwixt the constant red and mingled damask.
There be some women, Silvius, had they mark'd him
In parcels as I did, would have gone near
125 To fall in love with him: but, for my part,

overall irony ↗ ECH2 (handwritten)

Juxtaposition of what she did feel (heart) vs what she does feel (handwritten)

128 *what . . . do*: what cause had he.

129 *black*: i.e. not beautiful (according to Petrarchan conventions of beauty).

130 *am remember'd*: remind myself.

131 *I . . . again*: I didn't retort.

132 *all one*: doesn't matter.
Omittance . . . quittance: failure to rebuke him does not mean that I pardoned him ('quittance' = legal release from debt).

135 *straight*: immediately.

137 *passing short*: exceedingly curt.

I love him not nor hate him not—and yet
Have more cause to hate him than to love him.
For what had he to do to chide at me?
He said mine eyes were black, and my hair black,
130 And, now I am remember'd, scorn'd at me.
I marvel why I answer'd not again;
But that's all one. Omittance is no quittance. *[?me]*
I'll write to him a very taunting letter
And thou shalt bear it—wilt thou, Silvius?
    Silvius
135 Phoebe, with all my heart.
    Phoebe
                      I'll write it straight:
The matter's in my head and in my heart;
I will be bitter with him and passing short.
Go with me, Silvius.
                                    [Exeunt

ACT 4

Act 4 Scene 1
Disguised as Ganymede, Rosalind flirts with
Orlando.

SCENE 1

The forest: enter Rosalind *as* Ganymede, *and* Celia
as Aliena, *and* Jaques

Jaques
I prithee, pretty youth, let me be better acquainted with
thee.
    Rosalind
They say you are a melancholy fellow.
    Jaques
I am so: I do love it better than laughing.
    Rosalind
5 Those that are in extremity of either are abominable
fellows, and betray themselves to every modern censure
worse than drunkards.
    Jaques
Why, 'tis good to be sad and say nothing.
    Rosalind
Why then, 'tis good to be a post.
    Jaques
10 I have neither the scholar's melancholy, which is
emulation; nor the musician's, which is fantastical; nor
the courtier's, which is proud; nor the soldier's, which is
ambitious; nor the lawyer's, which is politic; nor the
lady's, which is nice; nor the lover's, which is all these;
15 but it is a melancholy of mine own, compounded of
many simples, extracted from many objects, and indeed
the sundry contemplation of my travels, in which my
often rumination wraps me in a most humorous
sadness.
    Rosalind
20 A traveller! By my faith, you have great reason to be sad.
I fear you have sold your own lands to see other men's.

5 *in extremity*: excessively.
6 *modern*: ordinary.

8 *sad*: serious.

9 *post*: 'As deaf as a post' is a common
comparison.

11 *emulation*: envy.
fantastical: imaginative,
temperamental.
13 *politic*: cunning, crafty.
14 *nice*: wanton, capricious.

16 *simples*: ingredients.
indeed: as a matter of fact.
17 *sundry . . . travels*: different things I
have seen when travelling.
17–19 *in . . . sadness*: and frequently
musing over these envelops me in a
very strange seriousness.

Then to have seen much and to have nothing is to have
rich eyes and poor hands.

Jaques

Yes, I have gained my experience.

Enter Orlando

Rosalind

25 And your experience makes you sad. I had rather have a
fool to make me merry than experience to make me
sad—and to travel for it too!

Orlando

Good day, and happiness, dear Rosalind.

Jaques

Nay then, God buy you, and you talk in blank verse!

Rosalind

30 Farewell, Monsieur Traveller. Look you lisp and wear
strange suits; disable all the benefits of your own
country; be out of love with your nativity, and almost
chide God for making you that countenance you are, or
I will scarce think you have swam in a gondola.

[*Exit* Jaques

35 Why, how now, Orlando, where have you been all this
while? You a lover? And you serve me such another
trick, never come in my sight more.

Orlando

My fair Rosalind, I come within an hour of my promise.

Rosalind

Break an hour's promise in love? He that will divide a
40 minute into a thousand parts and break but a part of
the thousand part of a minute in the affairs of love, it
may be said of him that Cupid hath clapped him
o'th'shoulder; but I'll warrant him heart-whole.

Orlando

Pardon me, dear Rosalind.

Rosalind

45 Nay, and you be so tardy, come no more in my sight—I
had as lief be wooed of a snail.

24 *Yes*: yes, but.

27 *travel*: Rosalind puns on 'travail'
(= labour).

29 *God buy you*: goodbye (see *3, 3, 233*
note).
and: if.
blank verse: Jaques is quick to notice
Orlando's pentameter.
30 *lisp*: speak with affectation.
31 *strange*: foreign.
disable: disparage.
benefits: natural advantages.
32 *nativity*: nationality.
34 *swam . . . gondola*: been conveyed in
a gondola, the chief mode of
transportation in Venice.

37 *trick*: action.

42–3 *Cupid . . . shoulder*: Cupid has
caught his attention (as a sergeant
arrests a criminal).
43 *warrant*: guarantee.
heart-whole: not wounded in the
heart.
46 *had as lief*: would rather.
of: by.

49 *jointure*: estate settled on a woman in case of her husband's death.
50 *his destiny*: i.e. to be made a cuckold; 'Cuckolds come by destiny' (proverbial).

52 *fain*: obliged.
53 *armed . . . fortune*: equipped with what he must acquire.
54 *prevents . . . wife*: anticipates the disgrace his wife will bring.
55 *horn-maker*: maker of cuckolds.

58 *leer*: complexion.

61 *very*: true, real.

64 *gravelled*: nonplussed, stuck (like a ship run aground).
   occasion: opportunity.
65 *are out*: have forgotten their speech.
66 *matter*: conversation.
67 *cleanliest shift*: smoothest tactic.

69 *entreaty*: pleading.

71 *out*: at a loss for words.

73 *my honesty . . . wit*: my (appearance of) chastity more abundant than my intelligence.

Orlando
Of a snail?
Rosalind
Aye, of a snail; for though he comes slowly, he carries his house on his head; a better jointure, I think, than you
50 make a woman. Besides, he brings his destiny with him.
Orlando
What's that?
Rosalind
Why, horns; which such as you are fain to be beholden to your wives for. But he comes armed in his fortune and prevents the slander of his wife.
Orlando
55 Virtue is no horn-maker, and my Rosalind is virtuous.
Rosalind
And I am your Rosalind.
Celia
It pleases him to call you so, but he hath a Rosalind of a better leer than you.
Rosalind
Come, woo me, woo me; for now I am in a holiday
60 humour and like enough to consent. What would you say to me now and I were your very, very Rosalind?
Orlando
I would kiss before I spoke.
Rosalind
Nay, you were better speak first, and when you were gravelled for lack of matter you might take occasion to
65 kiss. Very good orators when they are out, they will spit, and for lovers, lacking—God warrant us—matter, the cleanliest shift is to kiss.
Orlando
How if the kiss be denied?
Rosalind
Then she puts you to entreaty, and there begins new
70 matter.
Orlando
Who could be out, being before his beloved mistress?
Rosalind
Marry, that should you if I were your mistress, or I should think my honesty ranker than my wit.

74 *suit*: appeal, wooing.

75 *apparel . . . suit*: Rosalind puns on 'suit' = clothing.

79 *in her person*: speaking on her behalf.

81 *by attorney*: by proxy, have a lawyer act for you.
81–2 *poor . . . old*: Biblical scholars estimated this age for the world, which was thought to be decaying.
83 *died . . . person*: who died in real life. *videlicet*: namely.
84 *Troilus*: A Trojan prince who fell tragically in love with the Greek Cressida; Shakespeare used Chaucer's version of the story for his play *Troilus and Cressida*.
85 *die*: a) die for love; b) experience sexual orgasm.
86 *Leander*: A young man of Abydos who fell in love with Hero, a priestess of the temple of Venus in Sestos, on the opposite side of the Hellespont; he was drowned while swimming across to her in a tempest. Marlowe recounts some of this story in a narrative poem, *Hero and Leander* (quoted by Phoebe, 3, 6, 81).
87 *though*: even if.
91 *it*: the cause of death.
94 *right*: true.
   of this mind: thinking like this.
95 *protest*: declare.
97 *coming-on*: approachable.

Orlando

What, of my suit?

Rosalind

75 Not out of your apparel, and yet out of your suit. Am not I your Rosalind?

Orlando

I take some joy to say you are, because I would be talking of her.

Rosalind

Well, in her person, I say I will not have you.

Orlando

80 Then, in mine own person, I die.

Rosalind

No, faith, die by attorney. The poor world is almost six thousand years old and in all this time there was not any man died in his own person, videlicet, in a love-cause. Troilus had his brains dashed out with a Grecian club,

85 yet he did what he could to die before, and he is one of the patterns of love; Leander, he would have lived many a fair year though Hero had turned nun, if it had not been for a hot midsummer night, for, good youth, he went but forth to wash him in the Hellespont and, being

90 taken with the cramp, was drowned, and the foolish chroniclers of that age found it was Hero of Sestos. But these are all lies: men have died from time to time—and worms have eaten them—but not for love.

Orlando

I would not have my right Rosalind of this mind, for I

95 protest her frown might kill me.

Rosalind

By this hand, it will not kill a fly. But come, now I will be your Rosalind in a more coming-on disposition and, ask me what you will, I will grant it.

Orlando

Then love me, Rosalind.

Rosalind

100 Yes, faith, will I, Fridays and Saturdays and all.

Orlando

And wilt thou have me?

Rosalind

Aye, and twenty such.

Orlando

What sayest thou?

Rosalind

Are you not good?

Orlando

105   I hope so.

Rosalind

Why then, can one desire too much of a good thing?—
Come, sister, you shall be the priest and marry us.—
Give me your hand, Orlando.—What do you say, sister?

Orlando

Pray thee, marry us.

Celia

110   I cannot say the words.

Rosalind

You must begin: 'Will you, Orlando—'

Celia

Go to.—Will you, Orlando, have to wife this Rosalind?

Orlando

I will.

Rosalind

Aye, but when?

Orlando

115   Why, now, as fast as she can marry us.

Rosalind

Then you must say, 'I take thee, Rosalind, for wife.'

Orlando

I take thee, Rosalind, for wife.

Rosalind

I might ask you for your commission, but I do take thee,
Orlando, for my husband. There's a girl goes before the
120   priest, and certainly a woman's thought runs before her
actions.

Orlando

So do all thoughts: they are winged.

Rosalind

Now, tell me how long you would have her after you
have possessed her?

108   *Give . . . hand*: Rosalind seems to be enacting some kind of betrothal ceremony.

112   *Go to*: that's enough.

118   *commission*: authority.
119   *goes before*: anticipates.

124   *possessed her*: a) married her; b) had intercourse with her.

Orlando

125 For ever and a day.

Rosalind

Say a day without the 'ever'. No, no, Orlando: men are April when they woo, December when they wed; maids are May when they are maids, but the sky changes when they are wives. I will be more jealous of thee than a

130 Barbary cock-pigeon over his hen; more clamorous than a parrot against rain, more new-fangled than an ape; more giddy in my desires than a monkey. I will weep for nothing, like Diana in the fountain, and I will do that when you are disposed to be merry. I will laugh

135 like a hyena, and that when thou art inclined to sleep.

Orlando

But will my Rosalind do so?

Rosalind

By my life, she will do as I do.

Orlando

O, but she is wise.

Rosalind

Or else she could not have the wit to do this: the wiser,

140 the waywarder. Make the doors upon a woman's wit, and it will out at the casement; shut that, and 'twill out at the keyhole; stop that, 'twill fly with the smoke out at the chimney.

Orlando

A man that had a wife with such a wit, he might say,

145 'Wit, whither wilt?'

Rosalind

Nay, you might keep that check for it till you met your wife's wit going to your neighbour's bed.

Orlando

And what wit could wit have to excuse that?

Rosalind

Marry, to say she came to seek you there: you shall never

150 take her without her answer unless you take her without her tongue. O, that woman that cannot make her fault her husband's occasion, let her never nurse her child herself for she will breed it like a fool.

---

128 *when . . . maids*: while they are virgins.

130 *Barbary*: North African.
cock-pigeon: Male pigeons were said to be very possessive of their mates.
131 *against*: before.
new-fangled: fond of novelty.
132 *giddy*: changeable.
133 *Diana . . . fountain*: A possible reference to a fountain with a statue of Diana, goddess of chastity, which was erected in London in 1595.
135 *hyena*: A creature proverbial for its laughing sound.

140 *waywarder*: more wilful.
Make: bar, close.
141 *casement*: window.

145 *'Wit . . . wilt?'*: A proverbial saying (= where are your senses).

146 *check*: rebuke.

147 *wit*: sexual desire.

148 *what wit*: what ingenious excuse.

150 *take*: catch.

152 *her . . . occasion*: an opportunity to find fault with her husband.
nurse: breast-feed.
153 *breed*: raise, rear.

Orlando

For these two hours, Rosalind, I will leave thee.

Rosalind

155 Alas, dear love, I cannot lack thee two hours.

Orlando

I must attend the duke at dinner; by two o'clock I will be with thee again.

Rosalind

Aye, go your ways, go your ways. I knew what you would prove—my friends told me as much, and I
160 thought no less. That flattering tongue of yours won me. 'Tis but one cast away, and so come, Death! Two o'clock is your hour?

Orlando

Aye, sweet Rosalind.

Rosalind

By my troth, and in good earnest, and so God mend me,
165 and by all pretty oaths that are not dangerous, if you break one jot of your promise or come one minute behind your hour, I will think you the most pathetical break-promise, and the most hollow lover, and the most unworthy of her you call Rosalind that may be chosen
170 out of the gross band of the unfaithful. Therefore beware my censure, and keep your promise.

Orlando

With no less religion than if thou wert indeed my Rosalind. So adieu.

Rosalind

Well, Time is the old justice that examines all such
175 offenders, and let Time try. Adieu.   [*Exit* Orlando

Celia

You have simply misused our sex in your love-prate. We must have your doublet and hose plucked over your head, and show the world what the bird hath done to her own nest.

Rosalind

180 O coz, coz, coz, my pretty little coz, that thou didst know how many fathom deep I am in love! But it cannot be sounded: my affection hath an unknown bottom like the Bay of Portugal.

155 *lack*: be without.

156 *dinner*: the main midday meal.

158 *go your ways*: away with you.

161 *one . . . away*: one more woman deserted.

164 *troth*: faith.
      in . . . earnest: seriously.
      so God . . . me: may God improve me (proverbial).
165 *not dangerous*: Attempts were being made by religious reformers to suppress the use of blasphemous oaths.
166 *jot*: tiniest particle; the word derives from 'iota', the Greek 'i'.
167 *pathetical*: miserable, pitiable.
168 *hollow*: insincere.
170 *gross band*: whole company.
172 *religion*: devotion.

175 *try*: be the judge.

176 *simply misused*: utterly disgraced.
      love-prate: lover's chatter.
177–8 *plucked . . . head*: stripped off (like a servant unworthy of his uniform).
178–9 *bird . . . nest*: 'It is a foul bird that defiles its own nest' (proverbial).

181 *fathom*: A unit of depth (= six feet).
182 *sounded*: measured.
183 *Bay of Portugal*: Here the water is about 1400 fathoms deep.

Celia
Or rather bottomless, that as fast as you pour affection
185 in, it runs out.
Rosalind
No, that same wicked bastard of Venus that was begot of
thought, conceived of spleen, and born of madness, that
blind rascally boy that abuses everyone's eyes because
his own are out, let him be judge how deep I am in love.
190 I'll tell thee, Aliena, I cannot be out of the sight of
Orlando. I'll go find a shadow and sigh till he come.
Celia
And I'll sleep.   [*Exeunt*

186 *bastard of Venus*: Cupid; her lover
    (Mercury) and not her husband
    (Vulcan) was the father of Venus's son.
187 *thought*: fancy.
    spleen: impulse.
188 *blind*: 'Love is blind' (proverbial);
    Cupid is traditionally depicted as
    blind or blindfolded.
    abuses: deceives.
191 *shadow*: shady place.

Act 4 Scene 2
The lords celebrate their hunting success
(an interlude to occupy the two hours of
Orlando's attendance on the Duke at
dinner).

Scene 2

The forest: enter Jaques *and* Lords, Foresters *bearing
the antlers and skin of a deer*

Jaques
Which is he that killed the deer?
First Lord
Sir, it was I.
Jaques
Let's present him to the duke like a Roman conqueror—
and it would do well to set the deer's horns upon his
5 head for a branch of victory.—Have you no song,
forester, for this purpose?
First Forester
Yes, sir.
Jaques
Sing it. 'Tis no matter how it be in tune, so it make noise
enough.

Music

Song

Lords
10   What shall he have that kill'd the deer?
            His leather skin and horns to wear.

3 *like . . . conqueror*: i.e. with a
  victorious wreath on his head.
4–5 *deer's horns . . . victory*: The heads
  and horns of hunted animals were
  traditionally carried or hung up as
  trophies.

Then sing him home,
The rest shall bear this burden:

15

Take thou no scorn to wear the horn,
It was a crest ere thou wast born;
  Thy father's father wore it,
  And thy father bore it;
The horn, the horn, the lusty horn,
Is not a thing to laugh to scorn.   [*Exeunt*

SCENE 3

The forest: enter Rosalind *as* Ganymede *and* Celia *as*
Aliena

Rosalind
How say you now, is it not past two o'clock? And here
much Orlando!
  Celia
I warrant you, with pure love and troubled brain he
hath ta'en his bow and arrows and is gone forth—to
5 sleep. Look who comes here.

Enter Silvius *with a letter*

Silvius
My errand is to you, fair youth;
My gentle Phoebe did bid me give you this:
I know not the contents but, as I guess
By the stern brow and waspish action
10 Which she did use as she was writing of it,
It bears an angry tenor. Pardon me,
I am but as a guiltless messenger.
  Rosalind
[*After reading the letter*] Patience herself would startle
  at this letter
And play the swaggerer: bear this, bear all.
15 She says I am not fair, that I lack manners;
She calls me proud, and that she could not love me
Were man as rare as phoenix. Od's my will,
Her love is not the hare that I do hunt—

Left margin notes

13 *burden*: refrain.

14 *Take . . . scorn*: don't be ashamed.
the horn: The cuckold's horn now
seems to become an honourable sign
of manhood.
15 *crest*: heraldic device.
18 *lusty*: jolly, lustful.
19 *laugh . . . scorn*: make fun of. The
abrupt ending of the scene suggests
that some lines may be missing.

Act 4 Scene 3
Rosalind is amused to find that Phoebe has
fallen in love with 'Ganymede', but faints
when she hears that Orlando has been
injured.

2 *much*: not much.

4–5 *is . . . sleep*: has fallen asleep.

9 *waspish action*: spiteful gesture.

11 *tenor*: message.
12 *but as*: no more than.
13 *startle*: be alarmed.
14 *swaggerer*: quarrelsome fighter.
bear . . . all: if I can endure this, I can
endure anything (a common
catchphrase).
15 *fair*: beautiful.
16 *that*: states.
17 *phoenix*: a mythical Arabian bird; the
only one of its kind, it cremated itself
and a new bird rose from the ashes.
Od's my will: may God's will be done.

	Why writes she so to me? Well, shepherd, well?
20 *device*: invention.	20 This is a letter of your own device.
	Silvius
21 *protest*: declare.	No, I protest, I know not the contents;
	Phoebe did write it.
	Rosalind
	Come, come, you are a fool
23 *turn'd . . . love*: transformed into the most foolish kind of lover.	And turn'd into the extremity of love.
	I saw her hand, she has a leathern hand,
25 *freestone*: sandstone, limestone.	25 A freestone-colour'd hand. (I verily did think
verily: honestly.	That her old gloves were on, but 'twas her hands.)
27 *hussif*: housewife.	She has a hussif's hand—but that's no matter.
28 *invent*: compose.	I say she never did invent this letter:
29 *his hand*: a man's handwriting.	This is a man's invention and his hand.
	Silvius
	30 Sure, it is hers.
	Rosalind
	Why, 'tis a boisterous and a cruel style,
32 *defies*: challenges.	A style for challengers. Why, she defies me
33 *Like . . . Christian*: Christmas plays usually featured a Turkish knight who challenged a Christian knight in the name of 'Mahound'.	Like Turk to Christian. Woman's gentle brain
	Could not drop forth such giant-rude invention,
34 *drop forth*: give birth to.	35 Such Ethiop words, blacker in their effect
giant-rude: enormously insulting.	Than in their countenance. Will you hear the letter?
35 *Ethiop*: black as an African.	**Silvius**
	So please you, for I never heard it yet,
	Yet heard too much of Phoebe's cruelty.
	Rosalind
39 *She . . . me*: she addresses me with her own customary disdain.	She Phoebes me. Mark how the tyrant writes:
	40 [*Reads*] 'Art thou god to shepherd turn'd,
	That a maiden's heart hath burn'd?'
42 *rail*: scold.	Can a woman rail thus?
	Silvius
	Call you this railing?
	Rosalind
43 *laid apart*: set aside.	[*Reads*] 'Why, thy godhead laid apart,
47 *vengeance*: harm.	Warr'st thou with a woman's heart?'—
48 *Meaning . . . beast*: calling me an animal (since she says men could not injure her).	45 Did you ever hear such railing?—
	'Whiles the eye of man did woo me,
49–62 *'If . . . die'*: Phoebe declares her passion in the same conceits that she had scorned when Silvius used them (3, 6, 8–27).	That could do no vengeance to me.'—
	Meaning me a beast!
49 *eyne*: eyes (an archaic plural).	'If the scorn of your bright eyne

[Handwritten annotations: "degrading women" (near lines 32–33), "allusion" (near line 30), "irony" (near line 33)]

52 *in . . . aspect*: looking favourably (the phrase is astrological); 'aspect' is stressed on the second syllable.
53 *chid*: rebuked.
54 *move*: persuade.

57 *by . . . mind*: send a letter by him with your thoughts.
58 *kind*: natural affection.

60 *make*: earn.

65 *make thee*: use you as.
66 *strains*: pieces of music.

68 *snake*: drudge.

73 *purlieus*: borders.
74 *sheepcote*: shepherd's cottage.

75 *neighbour bottom*: water-meadow nearby.
76 *rank of osiers*: row of willow trees.
77 *Left . . . hand*: having left the 'osiers' on your right hand.
78 *keep*: guard.

50   Have power to raise such love in mine,
     Alack, in me what strange effect
     Would they work in mild aspect?
     Whiles you chid me, I did love;
     How then might your prayers move?
55   He that brings this love to thee
     Little knows this love in me;
     And by him seal up thy mind,
     Whether that thy youth and kind
     Will the faithful offer take
60   Of me and all that I can make,
     Or else by him my love deny,
     And then I'll study how to die.'

Silvius
Call you this chiding?
    Celia
                Alas, poor shepherd.
    Rosalind
Do you pity him? No, he deserves no pity.—Wilt thou
65 love such a woman? What, to make thee an instrument
and play false strains upon thee? Not to be endured!
Well, go your way to her—for I see love hath made thee
a tame snake—and say this to her: that if she love me, I
charge her to love thee; if she will not, I will never have
70 her, unless thou entreat for her. If you be a true lover,
hence, and not a word; for here comes more company.
                                            [*Exit* Silvius

Enter Oliver

Oliver
Good morrow, fair ones. Pray you, if you know
Where in the purlieus of this forest stands
A sheepcote fenc'd about with olive-trees.
    Celia
75 West of this place, down in the neighbour bottom;
The rank of osiers by the murmuring stream,
Left on your right hand, brings you to the place.
But at this hour the house doth keep itself:
There's none within.

Oliver

80 If that an eye may profit by a tongue,
Then should I know you by description:
Such garments, and such years. 'The boy is fair,
Of female favour, and bestows himself
Like a ripe sister; the woman low
85 And browner than her brother.' Are not you
The owners of the house I did enquire for?

Celia

It is no boast, being ask'd, to say we are.

Oliver

Orlando doth commend him to you both,
And to that youth he calls his Rosalind
90 He sends this bloody napkin. Are you he?

Rosalind

I am. What must we understand by this?

Oliver

Some of my shame, if you will know of me
What man I am, and how, and why, and where
This handkerchief was stain'd.

Celia

　　　　　　　　　　　　　I pray you tell it.

Oliver

95 When last the young Orlando parted from you,
He left a promise to return again
Within an hour and, pacing through the forest,
Chewing the food of sweet and bitter fancy,
Lo what befell. He threw his eye aside
100 And mark what object did present itself.
Under an old oak whose boughs were moss'd with age,
And high top bald with dry antiquity,
A wretched ragged man, o'ergrown with hair,
Lay sleeping on his back; about his neck
105 A green and gilded snake had wreath'd itself,
Who, with her head, nimble in threats, approach'd
The opening of his mouth. But suddenly
Seeing Orlando, it unlink'd itself
And with indented glides did slip away
110 Into a bush; under which bush's shade
A lioness, with udders all drawn dry,

80 *If . . . tongue*: if my eyes can understand what I have been told.

83 *favour*: feature.
bestows: behaves.
84 *ripe*: mature.
low: short.
85 *browner*: darker.

88 *commend him*: send greetings.

90 *napkin*: handkerchief.

92 *know of me*: let me tell you.

97 *Within an hour*: before very long.
98 *Chewing . . . fancy*: ruminating upon the oppositions of love (a favourite topic of Petrarchan love poetry).
99 *befell*: happened.
threw his eye: glanced.
102 *bald*: leafless.
105 *gilded*: yellow.
108 *unlink'd*: uncoiled.
109 *indented*: zigzag.

111 *drawn dry*: sucked dry by her cubs.

113 *When that*: to see when.
114 *royal*: Lions were monarchs of the animal kingdom.
119 *render him*: describe him as.

124 *purpos'd so*: intended to do so.
125 *kindness*: natural affection.
126 *occasion*: cause, reason.

128 *hurtling*: struggle.

131 *contrive*: plot.

132 *'Twas I . . . not I*: I was that man then, but I am not the same man now.
    do not shame: am not ashamed.

135 *for*: what about.

137 *our recountments*: the stories we had to tell.
    kindly: sweetly, naturally.
138 *As*: such as.
    desert: unpeopled.
139 *gentle*: noble.

Lay couching head on ground, with cat-like watch
When that the sleeping man should stir—for 'tis
The royal disposition of that beast
115 To prey on nothing that doth seem as dead.
This seen, Orlando did approach the man
And found it was his brother, his elder brother.
    Celia
O I have heard him speak of that same brother,
And he did render him the most unnatural
120 That liv'd amongst men.
    Oliver
                      And well he might do so,
For well I know he was unnatural.
    Rosalind
But to Orlando—did he leave him there,
Food to the suck'd and hungry lioness?
    Oliver
Twice did he turn his back and purpos'd so.
125 But kindness, nobler ever than revenge,
And nature, stronger than his just occasion,
Made him give battle to the lioness,
Who quickly fell before him; in which hurtling
From miserable slumber I awak'd.
    Celia
130 Are you his brother?
    Rosalind
                    Was't you he rescued?
    Celia
Was't you that did so oft contrive to kill him?
    Oliver
'Twas I, but 'tis not I. I do not shame
To tell you what I was, since my conversion
So sweetly tastes, being the thing I am.
    Rosalind
135 But for the bloody napkin?
    Oliver
                      By and by.
When from the first to last betwixt us two,
Tears our recountments had most kindly bath'd—
As how I came into that desert place—
In brief, he led me to the gentle duke

140 *array*: clothing.
     entertainment: nourishment.

147 *Brief*: in a few words.
     recover'd: revived.
148 *small space*: short time.
149 *as I am*: although I am.

156 *Cousin! Ganymede!*: Celia, in her
     fright, momentarily forgets their
     assumed names.

163 *a body*: anybody.
164 *counterfeited*: faked, pretended.

167 *complexion*: appearance.
     passion of earnest: genuine feeling.

140 Who gave me fresh array and entertainment,
     Committing me unto my brother's love,
     Who led me instantly unto his cave;
     There stripp'd himself and here, upon his arm,
     The lioness had torn some flesh away,
145 Which all this while had bled; and now he fainted,
     And cried in fainting upon Rosalind.
     Brief, I recover'd him, bound up his wound,
     And, after some small space, being strong at heart,
     He sent me hither, stranger as I am,
150 To tell this story that you might excuse
     His broken promise, and to give this napkin,
     Dyed in this blood, unto the shepherd youth
     That he in sport doth call his Rosalind.

         Rosalind *faints*

         Celia
     Why, how now? Ganymede, sweet Ganymede!
         Oliver
155 Many will swoon when they do look on blood.
         Celia
     There is more in it.—Cousin! Ganymede!
         Oliver
     [*Raising* Rosalind] Look, he recovers.
         Rosalind
     I would I were at home.
         Celia
     We'll lead you thither.—I pray you, will you take him by
160 the arm.
         Oliver
     Be of good cheer, youth. You a man? You lack a man's
     heart.
         Rosalind
     I do so, I confess it. Ah, sirrah, a body would think this
     was well counterfeited. I pray you tell your brother how
165 well I counterfeited. Heigh-ho!
         Oliver
     This was not counterfeit: there is too great testimony in
     your complexion that it was a passion of earnest.

Rosalind

Counterfeit, I assure you.

Oliver

Well then, take a good heart, and counterfeit to be a
170 man.

Rosalind

So I do. But, i'faith, I should have been a woman by
right.

Celia

Come, you look paler and paler: pray you, draw
homewards. Good sir, go with us.

Oliver

175 That will I. For I must bear answer back how you excuse
my brother, Rosalind.

Rosalind

I shall devise something. But I pray you commend my
counterfeiting to him. Will you go?   [*Exeunt*

173–4 *Come . . . us*: These are Celia's last
lines in the play, although she appears
in *Act 5*, Scene 4.
draw homewards: let's go home.

175 *excuse*: forgive.

177 *devise*: think of.

ACT 5

Act 5 Scene 1
Touchstone easily defeats William in a
dispute over Audrey's love.

SCENE 1

The forest: enter Touchstone *and* Audrey

Touchstone
We shall find a time, Audrey; patience, gentle Audrey.
Audrey
Faith, the priest was good enough, for all the old
gentleman's saying.
Touchstone
A most wicked Sir Oliver, Audrey, a most vile Martext.
5 But, Audrey, there is a youth here in the forest lays claim
to you.
Audrey
Aye, I know who 'tis. He hath no interest in me in the
world.

Enter William

Here comes the man you mean.
Touchstone
10 It is meat and drink to me to see a clown. By my troth,
we that have good wits have much to answer for. We
shall be flouting; we cannot hold.
William
Good ev'n, Audrey.
Audrey
God ye good ev'n, William.
William
15 [*Taking off his hat*] And good ev'n to you, sir.
Touchstone
Good ev'n, gentle friend. Cover thy head, cover thy
head. Nay prithee, be covered. How old are you, friend?
William
Five and twenty, sir.

2–3 *old gentleman*: i.e. Jaques.

7 *interest in*: legal right to.

10 *clown*: yokel, natural fool.
troth: faith.
11 *good wits*: keen intelligence.
12 *be flouting*: having a laugh.
hold: restrain ourselves.

13 *Good ev'n*: An address for any time of
day after noon.

14 *ye*: give you.

16 *Cover thy head*: put your hat on.

'But, Audrey, there is a youth here in the forest lays claim to you.' (*5*, 1, 5–6) Dearbhla Molloy as Audrey and Kenneth Branagh as Touchstone, Renaissance Theatre Company, 1988.

19 *ripe*: good, ready for marriage.

Touchstone

A ripe age. Is thy name William?

William

20 William, sir.

Touchstone

A fair name. Wast born i'th'forest here?

William

Aye, sir, I thank God.

Touchstone

'Thank God': a good answer. Art rich?

William

24 *so-so*: moderately; land-owning peasants at this time were increasingly prosperous.

Faith, sir, so-so.

Touchstone

25 'So-so' is good, very good, very excellent good—and yet it is not: it is but so-so. Art thou wise?

William

Aye, sir, I have a pretty wit.

Touchstone

Why, thou say'st well. I do now remember a saying: 'The fool doth think he is wise, but the wise man knows

30 himself to be a fool.'

William gapes

31–4 *The heathen . . . open*: Touchstone probably invents his 'philosopher' to confuse William who seems to be standing open-mouthed in wonder.

The heathen philosopher, when he had a desire to eat a grape, would open his lips when he put it into his mouth, meaning thereby that grapes were made to eat and lips to open. You do love this maid?

William

35 I do, sir.

Touchstone

36 *Give . . . hand*: Touchstone perhaps tries to trick William into thinking that he will perform some betrothal ceremony (compare *4*, 1, 108 note).

Give me your hand. Art thou learned?

William

No, sir.

Touchstone

38 *figure*: figure of speech.

Then learn this of me: to have is to have. For it is a figure in rhetoric that drink, being poured out of a cup into a

40 glass, by filling the one doth empty the other. For all

41 *your*: those well-known.
consent: agree together.
ipse: he (Latin).

your writers do consent that '*ipse*' is he. Now you are not *ipse*, for I am he.

act 2 scene 5 ✗

45 *vulgar*: vernacular.
46 *boorish*: the language of a boor (Touchstone's coinage).

50 *to wit*: that is to say.
   translate: convert.

52 *bastinado*: beating with a cudgel on the soles of the feet.
   in steel: with a sword.
53 *bandy . . . faction*: fight with you in a quarrel.
53–4 *o'errun . . . policy*: overwhelm you with craft.

William
Which he, sir?
   Touchstone
He, sir, that must marry this woman. Therefore, you
45 clown, abandon, which is in the vulgar 'leave', the
society, which in the boorish is 'company', of this
female, which in the common is 'woman': which
together is 'abandon the society of this female'; or,
clown, thou perishest or, to thy better understanding,
50 'diest', or, to wit, 'I kill thee', 'make thee away', 'translate
thy life into death, thy liberty into bondage'! I will deal
in poison with thee, or in bastinado, or in steel! I will
bandy with thee in faction, I will o'errun thee with
policy—I will kill thee a hundred and fifty ways!
55 Therefore, tremble and depart.
   Audrey
Do, good William.
   William
God rest you merry, sir.   [*Exit*

Enter Corin

   Corin
Our master and mistress seeks you. Come away, away.
   Touchstone
Trip, Audrey, trip, Audrey.—I attend, I attend.
                                            [*Exeunt*

Act 5 Scene 2
Oliver is now in love with 'Aliena', and Orlando agrees that he shall marry her. The lovers assemble, and 'Ganymede' promises that all shall get what they wish for.

2 *but*: only.

4 *persevere*: Stressed on the second syllable.
   enjoy: marry.
5 *giddiness*: rashness, impulsiveness.
5–6 *the . . . her*: her poverty (being without dowry).
6 *sudden*: hasty.

SCENE 2

The forest: enter Orlando *and* Oliver

   Orlando
Is't possible that on so little acquaintance you should
like her, that, but seeing, you should love her, and,
loving, woo, and, wooing, she should grant? And will
you persevere to enjoy her?
   Oliver
5 Neither call the giddiness of it in question, the poverty
of her, the small acquaintance, my sudden wooing, nor
her sudden consenting. But say with me I love Aliena;

8 *consent*: agree.

10 *revenue*: income.
11 *estate*: settle.

13–15 *You . . . followers*: Orlando
assumes the role of the bride's father.

17 *brother*: brother-in-law (as future
husband to 'Aliena').

18 *'sister'*: Perhaps Oliver is pretending
that 'Ganymede' is Orlando's
Rosalind—or perhaps he has seen
through the disguise.
20 *scarf*: sling.

27 *greater wonders*: i.e. Oliver's falling in
love with 'Aliena'.

28 *where you are*: what you mean.

30 *thrasonical*: vainglorious (like the
behaviour of Thraso, a braggart soldier
in a comedy by the Roman dramatist
Terence).
I came . . . overcame: Caesar's
boastful report to Rome was
frequently quoted ('*veni, vidi, vici*').

35 *degrees*: stages, steps.

say with her that she loves me; consent with both that
we may enjoy each other. It shall be to your good, for my
10 father's house and all the revenue that was old Sir
Roland's will I estate upon you, and here live and die a
shepherd.

Enter Rosalind *as* Ganymede

Orlando
You have my consent. Let your wedding be tomorrow;
thither will I invite the duke and all's contented
15 followers. Go you, and prepare Aliena, for look you,
here comes my 'Rosalind'.
Rosalind
God save you, brother.
Oliver
And you, fair 'sister'. [*Exit*
Rosalind
O, my dear Orlando, how it grieves me to see thee wear
20 thy heart in a scarf.
Orlando
It is my arm.
Rosalind
I thought thy heart had been wounded with the claws of
a lion.
Orlando
Wounded it is, but with the eyes of a lady.
Rosalind
25 Did your brother tell you how I counterfeited to swoon
when he showed me your handkerchief?
Orlando
Aye, and greater wonders than that.
Rosalind
O, I know where you are. Nay, 'tis true, there was never
anything so sudden but the fight of two rams, and
30 Caesar's thrasonical brag of 'I came, saw, and overcame.'
For your brother and my sister no sooner met but they
looked; no sooner looked, but they loved; no sooner
loved, but they sighed; no sooner sighed, but they asked
one another the reason; no sooner knew the reason, but
35 they sought the remedy; and in these degrees have they

36 *pair*: flight.
36–7 *climb incontinent*: ascend
   immediately.
37 *be incontinent*: be unchaste.
38 *wrath*: passion.
39 *clubs*: The weapons used to control
   rioters.
40 *bid*: invite.
   the duke: i.e. Duke Senior.

46 *turn*: needs.

49–50 *Know of me*: learn from me.
50 *to some purpose*: seriously.
51 *conceit*: understanding.
52 *that*: in order that.
53 *insomuch*: in that.

56 *grace me*: do me credit.
57 *strange*: wonderful.
58 *conversed*: associated.
   art: knowledge of magic.
59 *not damnable*: i.e. a practitioner of
   white, not black, magic.
59–60 *near the heart*: sincerely.
60 *gesture*: behaviour.
62 *straits*: circumstances.
63 *inconvenient*: inappropriate.
64–5 *human . . . danger*: in her own
   person and without any risk;
   communication with a phantom would
   indeed be 'damnable'.
66 *sober*: serious.
67 *tender dearly*: value highly.
67–8 *though . . . magician*: It was a
   capital offence to practise any kind of
   witchcraft.
68 *put . . . array*: put your best clothes
   on.
68–9 *bid your friends*: invite your family.

made a pair of stairs to marriage, which they will climb
incontinent—or else be incontinent before marriage.
They are in the very wrath of love, and they will
together—clubs cannot part them.

Orlando

40 They shall be married tomorrow and I will bid the duke
to the nuptial. But O, how bitter a thing it is to look into
happiness through another man's eyes. By so much the
more shall I tomorrow be at the height of heart-
heaviness, by how much I shall think my brother happy
45 in having what he wishes for.

Rosalind

Why then, tomorrow, I cannot serve your turn for
Rosalind?

Orlando

I can live no longer by thinking.

Rosalind

I will weary you then no longer with idle talking. Know
50 of me, then—for now I speak to some purpose—that I
know you are a gentleman of good conceit. I speak not
this that you should bear a good opinion of my
knowledge, insomuch, I say, I know you are; neither do
I labour for a greater esteem than may in some little
55 measure draw a belief from you to do yourself good,
and not to grace me. Believe then, if you please, that I
can do strange things. I have, since I was three year old,
conversed with a magician, most profound in his art,
and yet not damnable. If you do love Rosalind so near
60 the heart as your gesture cries it out, when your brother
marries Aliena shall you marry her. I know into what
straits of fortune she is driven, and it is not impossible
to me, if it appear not inconvenient to you, to set her
before your eyes tomorrow, human as she is, and
65 without any danger.

Orlando

Speak'st thou in sober meanings?

Rosalind

By my life, I do, which I tender dearly, though I say I am
a magician. Therefore, put you in your best array, bid
your friends. For if you will be married tomorrow, you
70 shall, and to Rosalind, if you will.

Enter Silvius *and* Phoebe

Look, here comes a lover of mine and a lover of hers.
Phoebe

72 *ungentleness*: discourtesy.

Youth, you have done me much ungentleness
To show the letter that I writ to you.
Rosalind

74 *study*: deliberate intention.

75 *despiteful*: spiteful.

I care not if I have. It is my study
75 To seem despiteful and ungentle to you.
You are there follow'd by a faithful shepherd;
Look upon him, love him: he worships you.
Phoebe
Good shepherd, tell this youth what 'tis to love.
Silvius
It is to be all made of sighs and tears,
80 And so am I for Phoebe.
Phoebe
And I for Ganymede.
Orlando
And I for Rosalind.
Rosalind
And I for no woman.
Silvius

84 *service*: devotion.

It is to be all made of faith and service,
85 And so am I for Phoebe.
Phoebe
And I for Ganymede.
Orlando
And I for Rosalind.
Rosalind
And I for no woman.
Silvius

89 *fantasy*: imagination.

90 *passion*: emotion.

91 *observance*: dutiful respect.

It is to be all made of fantasy,
90 All made of passion, and all made of wishes,
All adoration, duty, and observance,
All humbleness, all patience, and impatience,

93 *trial*: endurance.

All purity, all trial, all obedience.
And so am I for Phoebe.
Phoebe
95 And so am I for Ganymede.

98 *to love*: for loving.

106 *against*: at.

Orlando
And so am I for Rosalind.
    Rosalind
And so am I for no woman.
    Phoebe
[*To* Rosalind] If this be so, why blame you me to love
you?
    Silvius
100 [*To* Phoebe] If this be so, why blame you me to love
you?
    Orlando
If this be so, why blame you me to love you?
    Rosalind
Who do you speak to 'Why blame you me to love you'?
    Orlando
To her that is not here nor doth not hear.
    Rosalind
105 Pray you no more of this: 'tis like the howling of Irish
wolves against the moon. [*To* Silvius] I will help you, if
I can. [*To* Phoebe] I would love you, if I could.—
Tomorrow meet me all together.—[*To* Phoebe] I will
marry you, if ever I marry woman, and I'll be married
110 tomorrow. [*To* Orlando] I will satisfy you, if ever I
satisfy man, and you shall be married tomorrow. [*To*
Silvius] I will content you, if what pleases you contents
you, and you shall be married tomorrow. [*To* Orlando]
As you love Rosalind, meet; [*To* Silvius] as you love
115 Phoebe, meet—and as I love no woman, I'll meet. So
fare you well: I have left you commands.
    Silvius
I'll not fail, if I live.
    Phoebe
Nor I.
    Orlando
Nor I.   [*Exeunt*

Act 5 Scene 3
A little song to mark the passing of time.

SCENE 3

The forest: enter Touchstone *and* Audrey

Touchstone
Tomorrow is the joyful day, Audrey; tomorrow will we
be married.
   Audrey
I do desire it with all my heart, and I hope it is no
dishonest desire to desire to be a woman of the world?

Enter two Pages

5 Here come two of the banished duke's pages.
   First Page
Well met, honest gentleman.
   Touchstone
By my troth, well met. Come, sit, sit, and a song.
   Second Page
We are for you; sit i'th'middle.
   First Page
Shall we clap into't roundly, without hawking, or
10 spitting, or saying we are hoarse, which are the only
prologues to a bad voice?
   Second Page
Aye, faith, i'faith, and both in a tune like two gipsies on
a horse.
   First and Second Page
      It was a lover and his lass,
15   With a hey, and a ho, and a hey nonny-no,
      That o'er the green cornfield did pass,
         In spring-time,
            The only pretty ring-time,
               When birds do sing;
20   Hey ding-a-ding, ding
               Sweet lovers love the spring.

      Between the acres of the rye,
         With a hey, and a ho, and a hey nonny-no,
      These pretty country folks would lie,
25   In spring-time,

4 *dishonest*: unchaste.
   woman of the world: married woman.

6 *honest*: honourable.

8 *for you*: ready to serve you.
   i'th'middle: A reference to the rhyme
   'hey diddle diddle, fool in the middle'.
9 *clap into 't*: start singing briskly.
   hawking: clearing our throats.
10 *only*: principal.

12 *a tune*: unison.
   gipsies: These had a bad reputation as
   thieves and vagabonds.

14–45 *It was . . . spring*: For the music of
   this song see page 109.

18 *ring-time*: time for exchanging rings.

22 *Between . . . rye*: on the grass
   between the strips of corn.

The only pretty ring-time,
    When birds do sing;
Hey ding-a-ding, ding,
    Sweet lovers love the spring.

30 *carol*: song.

30 This carol they began that hour.
With a hey, and a ho, and a hey nonny-no,
How that a life was but a flower;
    In spring-time,
    The only pretty ring-time,
35   When birds do sing;
Hey ding-a-ding, ding,
    Sweet lovers love the spring.

38 *take . . . time*: make the most of the present moment.

And therefore take the present time;
With a hey, and a ho, and a hey nonny-no,

40 *crowned*: crownèd.
    prime: spring.

40 For love is crowned with the prime,
    In spring-time,
    The only pretty ring-time,
    When birds do sing;
Hey ding-a-ding, ding,
45   Sweet lovers love the spring.

Touchstone
Truly, young gentlemen, though there was no great
matter in the ditty, yet the note was very untunable.

47 *matter*: meaning.
    note: tune.

First Page
You are deceived, sir: we kept time; we lost not our time.

48 *lost not*: did not get out of.

Touchstone
By my troth, yes. I count it but time lost to hear such a

49 *time lost*: a waste of time.

50 *mend*: improve.

50 foolish song. God buy you, and God mend your
voices.—Come, Audrey.   [*Exeunt*

Act 5 Scene 4
The lovers assemble in the Forest meeting-place: all is revealed, the weddings are celebrated by Hymen, and Duke Senior with his lords can return to the court.

1 *the boy*: i.e. 'Ganymede'.
2 *promised*: promisèd.

4 *fear . . . fear*: are afraid that their hopes are unfounded, and know that they are afraid their hopes will not be fulfilled.

5 *compact*: covenant, agreement. *urg'd*: repeated.

7 *bestow her*: give her in marriage.

18 *make . . . even*: straighten everything out.

Scene 4

The forest: enter Duke Senior, Amiens, Jaques, Orlando, Oliver, Celia *as* Aliena

Duke Senior
Dost thou believe, Orlando, that the boy
Can do all this that he hath promised?
Orlando
I sometimes do believe and sometimes do not,
As those that fear they hope and know they fear.

Enter Rosalind *as* Ganymede, Silvius, *and* Phoebe

Rosalind
5 Patience once more whiles our compact is urg'd.—
You say, if I bring in your Rosalind,
You will bestow her on Orlando here?
Duke Senior
That would I, had I kingdoms to give with her.
Rosalind
And you say you will have her, when I bring her?
Orlando
10 That would I, were I of all kingdoms king.
Rosalind
You say you'll marry me, if I be willing.
Phoebe
That will I, should I die the hour after.
Rosalind
But if you do refuse to marry me,
You'll give yourself to this most faithful shepherd.
Phoebe
15 So is the bargain.
Rosalind
You say that you'll have Phoebe if she will.
Silvius
Though to have her and death were both one thing.
Rosalind
I have promis'd to make all this matter even.—
Keep you your word, O duke, to give your daughter.—
20 You yours, Orlando, to receive his daughter.—

Keep your word, Phoebe, that you'll marry me
Or else, refusing me, to wed this shepherd.—
Keep your word, Silvius, that you'll marry her
If she refuse me—and from hence I go
25 To make these doubts all even.

[*Exeunt* Rosalind *and* Celia

Duke Senior
I do remember in this shepherd boy
Some lively touches of my daughter's favour.
    Orlando
My lord, the first time that I ever saw him,
Methought he was a brother to your daughter;
30 But, my good lord, this boy is forest-born
And hath been tutor'd in the rudiments
Of many desperate studies by his uncle
Whom he reports to be a great magician,
Obscured in the circle of this forest.

Enter Touchstone *and* Audrey

    Jaques
35 There is sure another flood toward, and these couples
are coming to the ark. Here comes a pair of very strange
beasts which, in all tongues, are called fools.
    Touchstone
Salutation and greeting to you all.
    Jaques
Good my lord, bid him welcome. This is the motley-
40 minded gentleman that I have so often met in the forest:
he hath been a courtier, he swears.
    Touchstone
If any man doubt that, let him put me to my purgation.
I have trod a measure; I have flattered a lady; I have
been politic with my friend, smooth with mine enemy;
45 I have undone three tailors; I have had four quarrels,
and like to have fought one.
    Jaques
And how was that ta'en up?
    Touchstone
Faith, we met and found the quarrel was upon the
seventh cause.

27 *lively touches*: lifelike traits.
    favour: features.

31 *rudiments*: first principles.
32 *desperate*: dangerous (see 5, 2, 67–8
    note).
34 *Obscured . . . circle*: obscurèd; hidden
    within the boundaries (as in a
    magician's magic circle).
35 *another flood*: i.e. like the universal
    flood described in Genesis.
    toward: about to happen.
35–6 *these . . . ark*: God told Noah to
    shelter the beasts 'by couples, the
    male and his female', in the ark.

42 *purgation*: test.
43 *measure*: stately dance.
44 *politic*: hypocritical.
    smooth: deceptively courteous.
45 *undone*: ruined (by not paying their
    bills).
46 *like . . . fought*: almost had to fight
    over.
47 *ta'en up*: settled.
48–9 *the seventh cause*: Touchstone
    explains this in lines 64–95.

52 *God'ild you*: may God reward you.
   desire . . . like: return the
   compliment.
53 *country copulatives*: country folk
   about to be coupled in marriage.
53–4 *swear . . . forswear*: make vows and
   break them.
54 *marriage binds*: the marriage bond
   fastens us together.
54–5 *blood breaks*: desire breaks the
   bond.
55 *ill-favoured*: ugly.
56 *humour*: whim, fancy.
57 *honesty*: virtue, chastity.
58 *pearl . . . oyster*: 'Rich pearls are
   found in homely shells' (proverbial).
59 *swift*: witty.
   sententious: full of wise sayings.
60 *bolt*: arrow, wit; 'A fool's bolt is soon
   shot (= blunted)' (proverbial).
60–1 *dulcet diseases*: sweet weaknesses;
   perhaps Touchstone considers the
   cliché to be a linguistic disease.
64–77 *Upon . . . direct*: Shakespeare
   satirizes the many trivial offences,
   strictly defined, that might give
   occasion for a duel.
65 *dislike*: adversely criticize.
67 *in the mind*: of the opinion.
69 *again*: in reply.
71 *modest*: moderate.
   disabled: disparaged, belittled.
75 *countercheck*: rebuke.
76 *circumstantial*: contradiction given
   indirectly depending on
   circumstances.
80–1 *measured swords*: Swords were
   measured before a duel to check that
   they were of equal length.

Jaques
50 How, 'seventh cause'?—Good my lord, like this fellow.
   Duke Senior
   I like him very well.
   Touchstone
   God'ild you, sir; I desire you of the like. I press in here,
   sir, amongst the rest of the country copulatives, to swear
   and to forswear according as marriage binds and blood
55 breaks. A poor virgin, sir, an ill-favoured thing, sir, but
   mine own. A poor humour of mine, sir, to take that that
   no man else will. Rich honesty dwells like a miser, sir, in
   a poor house, as your pearl in your foul oyster.
   Duke Senior
   By my faith, he is very swift and sententious.
   Touchstone
60 According to 'the fool's bolt', sir, and such dulcet
   diseases.
   Jaques
   But, for 'the seventh cause': how did you find the
   quarrel on 'the seventh cause'?
   Touchstone
   Upon a lie seven times removed.—Bear your body
65 more seeming, Audrey.—As thus, sir: I did dislike the
   cut of a certain courtier's beard. He sent me word, if I
   said his beard was not cut well, he was in the mind it
   was: this is called 'the retort courteous'. If I sent him
   word again it was not well cut, he would send me word
70 he cut it to please himself: this is called 'the quip
   modest'. If again it was not well cut, he disabled my
   judgement: this is called 'the reply churlish'. If again it
   was not well cut, he would answer I spake not true: this
   is called 'the reproof valiant'. If again it was not well cut,
75 he would say I lied: this is called 'the countercheck
   quarrelsome'. And so to 'the lie circumstantial' and 'the
   lie direct'.
   Jaques
   And how oft did you say his beard was not well cut?
   Touchstone
   I durst go no further than the lie circumstantial, nor he
80 durst not give me the lie direct; and so we measured
   swords, and parted.

82 *nominate*: name.

83 *in print*: according to the book of
   rules.
84 *books . . . manners*: Such 'courtesy
   books' were popular at this time, when
   correct behaviour was most important.

88 *circumstance*: circumlocution,
   indirect proceeding.

90 *knew*: have known.

91 *take up*: resolve.

93 *thought but*: simply thought.
   as: namely.
94 *swore brothers*: swore a joint oath.
95 *only*: unique.

98 *stalking-horse*: horse trained to
   conceal hunters as they moved
   towards their prey.
99 *presentation*: display.
   wit: witticisms.
99s.d. *Still*: soft.
   Hymen: The Roman god of marriage
   (usually bearing a torch, and
   sometimes descending on a throne
   from above the stage).

101 *made even*: reconciled.
102 *Atone*: harmonize.

107 *Whose*: i.e. Rosalind's; the
   interchange of lovers' hearts was a
   common poetic conceit.

Jaques
Can you nominate, in order now, the degrees of the lie?
   Touchstone
O, sir, we quarrel in print, by the book—as you have
books for good manners. I will name you the degrees:
85 the first, the retort courteous; the second, the quip
modest; the third, the reply churlish; the fourth, the
reproof   valiant;   the   fifth,   the   countercheck
quarrelsome; the sixth, the lie with circumstance; the
seventh, the lie direct. All these you may avoid but the
90 lie direct, and you may avoid that too with an 'if'. I knew
when seven justices could not take up a quarrel but,
when the parties were met themselves, one of them
thought but of an 'if': as, 'If you said so, then I said so.'
And they shook hands and swore brothers. Your 'if' is
95 the only peacemaker: much virtue in 'if'.
   Jaques
Is not this a rare fellow, my lord? He's as good at
anything, and yet a fool.
   Duke Senior
He uses his folly like a stalking-horse, and under the
presentation of that he shoots his wit.

Still music. Enter Hymen, *with* Rosalind *and* Celia *as
themselves*

   Hymen
100   Then is there mirth in heaven,
         When earthly things made even
            Atone together.
         Good duke, receive thy daughter;
         Hymen from heaven brought her,
105   Yea, brought her hither
         That thou might'st join her hand with his,
         Whose heart within his bosom is.
   Rosalind
[*To the* Duke] To you I give myself, for I am yours.
[*To* Orlando] To you I give myself, for I am yours.
   Duke Senior
110 If there be truth in sight, you are my daughter.

'Here's eight that must take hands To join in Hymen's bands' (5, 4, 119–20). Ian Hogg as Duke Senior, Tom Smith as Oliver, Nancy Carroll as Celia, Peter Copley as Hymen, Anthony Howell as Orlando, and Alexandra Gilbreath as Rosalind, Royal Shakespeare Company, 2000.

Orlando
If there be truth in sight, you are my Rosalind.
Phoebe

112 *shape*: appearance.

If sight and shape be true, why then, my love, adieu.
Rosalind
[*To the* Duke] I'll have no father, if you be not he.
[*To* Orlando] I'll have no husband, if you be not he.
115 [*To* Phoebe] Nor ne'er wed woman, if you be not she.
Hymen

116 *bar*: forbid.

Peace, ho: I bar confusion,
'Tis I must make conclusion
Of these most strange events.
Here's eight that must take hands

120 *bands*: bonds (of marriage).
121 *If . . . contents*: if, now the truth is known, it brings true happiness.
122 *cross*: quarrel.

120 To join in Hymen's bands,
If truth holds true contents.
[*To* Orlando *and* Rosalind] You and you no cross shall part.
[*To* Oliver *and* Celia] You and you are heart in heart.

124 *accord*: agree.

[*To* Phoebe] You to his love must accord,
125 Or have a woman to your lord.

126 *sure*: united.

[*To* Touchstone *and* Audrey] You and you are sure together
As the winter to foul weather.—

128 *Whiles*: until.

Whiles a wedlock hymn we sing,
Feed yourselves with questioning,

130 *reason . . . diminish*: the explanations can reduce the surprise.

130 That reason, wonder may diminish
How thus we met and these things finish.

Song

132 *Juno's crown*: the crown bestowed (or worn) by Juno, goddess of marriage.
133 *board and bed*: i.e. the complete marital relationship.
134 *Hymen*: marriage.
peoples: populates.
135 *High*: solemn, ceremonial (or, possibly, 'let wedlock be highly honoured').
honoured: honourèd.

Wedding is great Juno's crown,
O blessed bond of board and bed.
'Tis Hymen peoples every town,
135 High wedlock then be honoured.
Honour, high honour, and renown
To Hymen, god of every town.
Duke Senior
O my dear niece: welcome thou art to me

139 *Even daughter*: as though you were my daughter.

Even daughter; welcome in no less degree.

Phoebe
140 I will not eat my word now thou art mine:
Thy faith my fancy to thee doth combine.

Enter Jacques de Boys, *the second brother*

Jacques de Boys
Let me have audience for a word or two.
I am the second son of old Sir Roland,
That bring these tidings to this fair assembly.
145 Duke Frederick, hearing how that every day
Men of great worth resorted to this forest,
Address'd a mighty power which were on foot
In his own conduct, purposely to take
His brother here and put him to the sword;
150 And to the skirts of this wild wood he came,
Where, meeting with an old religious man,
After some question with him, was converted
Both from his enterprise and from the world,
His crown bequeathing to his banish'd brother,
155 And all their lands restor'd to them again
That were with him exil'd. This to be true,
I do engage my life.
Duke Senior
                                    Welcome, young man.
Thou offer'st fairly to thy brother's wedding:
To one his lands withheld, and to the other
160 A land itself at large, a potent dukedom.—
First, in this forest, let us do those ends
That here were well begun and well begot;
And, after, every of this happy number
That have endur'd shrewd days and nights with us
165 Shall share the good of our returned fortune
According to the measure of their states.
Meantime forget this new-fall'n dignity
And fall into our rustic revelry.—
Play, music—and, you brides and bridegrooms all,
170 With measure heap'd in joy to th'measures fall.
Jaques
Sir, by your patience. [*To* Jacques de Boys] If I heard
  you rightly,

141 *my fancy . . . combine*: binds my love to you.

144 *tidings*: news.

146 *great worth*: high rank.
147 *Address'd*: prepared.
147–8 *were . . . conduct*: had set out under his own command.

150 *skirts*: edges.
151 *religious man*: hermit.
152 *question*: discussion.
153 *the world*: all worldly things.

157 *engage*: pledge.
158 *offer'st fairly*: bring fine gifts.
159 *To . . . withheld*: Orlando in fact already knows that Oliver has restored his lands (*5, 2, 10–11*).
to the other: i.e. to himself.
160 *at large*: entire.
potent: powerful.
161 *do . . . ends*: fulfil those intentions.
163 *every*: every one.
164 *shrewd*: sharp, hard.
165 *returned*: returnèd.
166 *According . . . states*: in proportion to the nature of their ranks; the old hierarchies are already being restored after the apparent equalities of the Forest.
167 *new-fall'n dignity*: recently acquired honour.
170 *measure . . . joy*: cup overflowing with happiness.
to . . . fall: join in the (formal) dancing.
171 *by your patience*: just a moment, please.

173 *thrown . . . court*: abandoned
ceremonious court life.

The duke hath put on a religious life
And thrown into neglect the pompous court.
    Jacques de Boys
He hath.
    Jaques

175 *will I*: I will go.
out . . . convertites: from these
religious converts.
176 *matter*: good sense.
177 *bequeath*: entrust.

175 To him will I: out of these convertites
There is much matter to be heard and learn'd.
[*To the* Duke] You to your former honour I bequeath:
Your patience and your virtue well deserves it.
[*To* Orlando] You to a love that your true faith doth
    merit.

180 *allies*: relatives.
181 *well-deserved*: deservèd.
182 *wrangling*: quarrelling.

180 [*To* Oliver] You to your land and love and great allies.
[*To* Silvius] You to a long and well-deserved bed.
[*To* Touchstone] And you to wrangling, for thy loving
    voyage

183 *victuall'd*: supplied with food.

Is but for two months victuall'd.—So to your
    pleasures;
I am for other than for dancing measures.
    Duke Senior

185 Stay, Jaques, stay.
    Jaques

186 *pastime*: frivolity.
would have: desire.
187 *stay*: wait.

To see no pastime, I. What you would have
I'll stay to know at your abandon'd cave.   [*Exit*
    Duke Senior
Proceed, proceed.—We will begin these rites
As we do trust they'll end, in true delights.

    They dance

        [*Exeunt all but* Rosalind

Epilogue

The boy actor's farewell.

1 *to see . . . Epilogue*: to have the Epilogue spoken by a female character.
2 *unhandsome*: unbecoming.
  to see . . . Prologue: to have lords going before ladies.
4–5 *good . . . bush*: The saying was proverbial, referring to the bush or garland hung as advertisement outside an inn or a vintner's shop.
6 *case*: state.
7 *insinuate*: ingratiate myself.
8 *furnished*: costumed.
10 *conjure*: a) solemnly enjoin; b) charm—as though Rosalind were the magician she claimed to be in *5, 2, 67–8*.

14 *simpering*: smirking, smiling.
15–16 *If I were a woman*: The boy actor, probably still wearing Rosalind's costume, draws attention to his gender for the last time.
17 *liked*: pleased.
18 *defied*: disliked.

20 *offer*: i.e. to kiss the spectators.
  bid me farewell: applaud me.

EPILOGUE

Rosalind

It is not the fashion to see the lady the Epilogue, but it is no more unhandsome than to see the lord the Prologue. If it be true that good wine needs no bush, 'tis true that a good play needs no Epilogue. Yet to good wine they do
5 use good bushes, and good plays prove the better by the help of good Epilogues. What a case am I in, then, that am neither a good Epilogue nor cannot insinuate with you in the behalf of a good play? I am not furnished like a beggar, therefore to beg will not become me. My way
10 is to conjure you, and I'll begin with the women. I charge you, O women, for the love you bear to men, to like as much of this play as please you.—And I charge you, O men, for the love you bear to women—as I perceive by your simpering none of you hates them—
15 that between you and the women the play may please. If I were a woman, I would kiss as many of you as had beards that pleased me, complexions that liked me, and breaths that I defied not. And I am sure as many as have good beards, or good faces, or sweet breaths will, for my
20 kind offer, when I make curtsy, bid me farewell.

[*Exit*

IT WAS A LOVER AND HIS LASS

'It was a lover and his lass' (*Act 5*, Scene 3)

A musical setting for this attractive lyric is to be found in Thomas
Morley's *First Book of Airs*, published in 1600.

o'er   the   green   corn - fields   did   pass,
pret - ty   coun - try   fools   would   lie,   } In   Spring   time,   in
that   a   life   was   but   a   flower,
love   is   crown - ed   with   the   prime,

Spring   time, in   Spring   time, the   on - ly   pret - ty   ring - time, When

birds   do   sing   hey   ding a ding a ding,   hey   ding a ding a ding, hey

ding a ding a ding Sweet lov - ers love the Spring, in Spring

time,   in Spring time, the on - ly pret - ty ring time, When

birds do sing hey ding a ding a ding, hey ding a ding a ding, hey

ding a ding a ding, Sweet lov - ers love the Spring.

Classwork and Examinations

The works of Shakespeare are studied all over the world, and this classroom edition is being used in many different countries. Teaching methods vary from school to school—even *within* the United Kingdom—and there are many different ways of examining a student's work. Some teachers and examiners expect detailed knowledge of Shakespeare's text; others ask for imaginative involvement with his characters and their situations; and there are some teachers who want their students, by means of 'workshop' activities, to share in the theatrical experience of directing and performing a play. Most people use a variety of methods. This section of the book offers a few suggestions for approaches to *As You Like It* which could be used in schools and colleges to help with students' understanding and *enjoyment* of the play.

A Discussion of Themes and Topics
B Character Study
C Activities
D Context Questions
E Critical Appreciation
F Essays
G Projects

A Discussion of Themes and Topics

It is most sensible to discuss each scene as it is read, sharing impressions (and perhaps correcting misapprehensions): no two people experience any character in quite the same way, and we all have different expectations. It can be useful to compare aspects of this play with other fictions—plays, novels, films—or with modern life. A large class should divide into small groups, each with a leader, who can discuss different aspects of a single topic and then report back to the main assembly.

Suggestions

A1 When Rosalind and Celia are invited to watch the wrestling in *Act 1*, Scene 2, Touchstone observes 'it is the first time that ever I heard breaking of ribs was sport for ladies' (121–2). Do you agree with his attitude?

A2 Celia is surprised when Rosalind declares her feelings for Orlando: 'Is it possible, on such a sudden, you should fall into so strong a liking?' (1, 3, 24–5). Do *you* believe in love at first sight?

A3 In the forest of Arden, Duke Senior addresses his followers:

> shall we go and kill us venison?
> And yet it irks me the poor dappled fools,
> Being native burghers of this desert city,
> Should, in their own confines, with forked heads
> Have their round haunches gor'd.   (2, 1, 21–5)

How do you react to this speech?

A4 Duke Senior asserts that the simple life in the Forest of Arden is 'more sweet Than that of painted pomp' (2, 1, 2–3). What is your idea of the Good Life?

A5 By 'courtesy of nations' (1, 1, 41) the eldest son inherits all. Is this fair?

A6 Would anything be gained—or lost—by staging this play in modern dress?

A7 Discuss the social functions of satire in the light of Jaques' comments (2, 7, 45–87). Is there any modern equivalent for the court fool?

B Character Study Shakespeare's characters can be studied in many different ways, either from the *outside*, where the detached, critical student (or group of students) can see the function of every character within the whole scheme and pattern of the play; or from the *inside*, where the sympathetic student (like an actor) can identify with a single character and can look at the action and the other characters from his/her point of view.

a) from 'outside' the character

B1 Compare the characters of
a) Rosalind and Celia
b) Duke Senior and Duke Frederick
c) Oliver and Orlando

B2 Discuss the characters and dramatic functions of
a) Jaques
b) Touchstone
c) Adam

B3 Compare Orlando and Silvius as romantic lovers.

B4 Why do you think that Shakespeare introduces the truly rural characters—Corin, Audrey, and William—into this pastoral fantasy?

B5 'Not one of the characters in *As You Like It* is truly credible: their passions are always too extreme.' Do you agree?

b) from 'inside' a character

B6 As Orlando, give an account of your young life, filling in the details of your brother's harsh treatment.

B7 Give full media coverage—newspaper, radio, television—to the wrestling matches in *Act 1*, Scene 2, being very sure to get interviews with Charles, the chief wrestler, and with people who hold strong views about such 'sports'.

B8 Write Adam's memoirs of his service with 'old Sir Roland'.

B9

> All the world's a stage,
> And all the men and women merely players:
> They have their exits and their entrances
> And one man in his time plays many parts,
> His acts being seven ages.

2, 7, 139–143

Jaques proceeds to describe 'the Seven Ages of Man'. Write 'the Seven Ages of Woman'.

B10 Celia gives—1, 3, 68–71—a very succinct account of her friendship with Rosalind. Describe the relationship with *your* best friend.

B11 Re-write Orlando's verses—*Act 3*, Scene 2—in a modern idiom.

B12 In Celia's diary describe your observation of Rosalind's love affair with Orlando.

B13 In the character of Audrey, (*a*) tell your parents about Touchstone and your woodland 'marriage' in *Act 3*, Scene 4; (*b*) talk to William about your marriage to Touchstone which may—or may not—have been 'but for two months victual'd' (5, 4, 183).

B14 Write a letter from Phoebe to her girlfriend, telling her all about Silvius and her meeting with 'Ganymede'.

B15 In Orlando's diary, confide your feelings after the mock marriage (*Act 4*, Scene 1) with the boy whom you called 'Rosalind'.

B16 The reformed Oliver identifies himself to Rosalind, saying

> I do not shame
> To tell you what I was, since my conversion
> So sweetly tastes, being the thing I am. $\qquad$ 4, 3, 132–4

In Oliver's diary (or letter to his friend), reveal all the stages in your 'conversion'.

B17 Recount the events of *Act 5*, Scene 4 as seen through the eyes of
a) Duke Senior
b) Orlando
c) Silvius
d) Phoebe

B18 We are told (5, 4, 145–56) how Duke Frederick followed his brother into the Forest of Arden.

> Where, meeting with an old religious man,
> After some question with him, [he] was converted.

Write the Duke's story, *either* as an intimate letter to a close friend, *or* for publication as a feature-article: ' "Why I renounced the world": thoughts of a ducal drop-out'.

B19 'Where are they now?' Celia, former head girl of Arden High School, writes for the school magazine describing events leading up to the double marriage.

B20 Several Lords followed Duke Senior into the Forest of Arden (where they could 'fleet the time carelessly, as they did in the golden world', 1, 1, 108–9). As one of these Lords, explain your action to the wife or friends you left at court; describe your life in the Forest and your feelings about your return.

C   Activities   These can involve two or more students, preferably working *away from* the desk or study-table and using gesture and position ('body-language') as well as speech. They can help students to develop a sense of drama and the dramatic aspects of Shakespeare's play—which was written to be *performed*, not studied in a classroom.

Suggestions   **C1**   Speak the lines—act the scenes! To familiarize yourselves with Shakespeare's verse, try different reading techniques—reading by punctuation marks (where each person hands over to the next at every punctuation mark); reading by sentences; and reading by speeches.

Begin acting with small units—about ten lines—where two or three characters are speaking to each other; rehearse these in groups of students, and perform them before the whole class. Read the lines from a script—then act them out in your own words.

C2 Organize a 'town *versus* country' debate between those who share Duke Senior's views and those who take sides with Touchstone (see 2, 1, 2–4 *and* 2, 4, 13–14)

> Hath not old custom made this life more sweet
> Than that of painted pomp? Are not these woods
> More fee from peril than the envious court?

and

> '...now I am in Arden, the more fool I! When I was at
> home, I was in a better place'.

C3 Produce a holiday brochure or television commercial for Duke's Travel Agency Forest Retreats (perhaps with special discounts for senior citizens).

C4
> When it comes, will it come without warning
>   Just as I'm picking my nose?
> Will it knock on my door in the morning,
>   Or tread in the bus on my toes?
> Will it come like a change in the weather?
>   Will its greeting be courteous or rough?
> Will it alter my life altogether?
>   O tell me the truth about love.

> (W.H. Auden, Song XII)

Organize a classroom debate to answer Auden's question. How would the question be answered by the different characters in *As You Like It*?

C5 Orlando's verses have been re-written in modern idiom (see B11). Devise a scene in which they are discussed by modern Rosalind and Celia.

D Context Questions Questions like these, which are sometimes used in written examinations, can also be helpful as a class revision quiz, testing knowledge of the play and some understanding of its words.

D1 Good my complexion, dost thou think, though I am caparisoned like a man, I have a doublet and hose in my disposition? One inch of delay more is a South Sea of discovery. I prithee tell me who is it—quickly, and speak apace.

    (i)   Who is the speaker? Who is referred to?

   (ii)   Why is the speaker 'caparisoned like a man'? What name does she use when she is appearing as a man?

  (iii)   Who comes on to the stage after this speech? What does the speaker offer to do?

D2   He threw his eye aside
And mark what object did present itself.
Under an old oak whose boughs were moss'd with age,
And high top bald with dry antiquity,
A wretched ragged man, o'ergrown with hair,
Lay sleeping on his back.

    (i)   Who is the speaker? To whom does he speak?

   (ii)   Who are the two men referred to in the passage?

  (iii)   What happened when the sleeping man awoke? What effect does this story have on one of the hearers?

D3   I remember when I was in love. I broke my sword upon a stone, and bid him take that for coming a-night to Jane Smile; and I remember the kissing of her batler, and the cow's dugs that her pretty chopt hands had milked.

    (i)   Who is speaking? To whom is he speaking?

   (ii)   Why is the speaker in his present situation?

  (iii)   What two persons have reminded the speaker of the time when he was in love?

D4   Then but forbear your food a little while,
Whiles, like a doe, I go to find my fawn,
And give it food: there is an old poor man,
Who after me hath many a weary step
Limp'd in pure love.

    (i)   Who is compared to the doe, and who is the fawn?

   (ii)   Why has the old man accompanied the speaker, and why has the speaker made this journey?

  (iii)   To whom are these lines addressed? Why are they in this place?

D5   But let your fair eyes and gentle wishes go with me to my trial, wherein if I be foiled, there is but one shamed that was never gracious; if killed, but one dead that is willing to be so.

    (i)   Who is the speaker? Whose are the 'fair eyes and gentle
           wishes'?
    (ii)   What is the 'trial' that is mentioned? What is the result of
           this trial?
    (iii) Why is the speaker willing to be dead? How do we know
           that he is in more danger than he suspects?

D6 Neither call the giddiness of it in question, the poverty of her, the
small acquaintance, my sudden wooing, nor her sudden consenting.
But say with me, I love—; say with her that she loves me; consent with
both that we may enjoy each other.

    (i)   Who is speaking? To whom does he speak?
    (ii)   What does he call the woman he loves? What is her real
           name?
    (iii) What does he offer to the person addressed?

D7 And will you, being a man of your breeding, be married under a
bush like a beggar? Get you to church, and have a good priest that can
tell you what marriage is. This fellow will but join you together as they
join wainscot; then one of you will prove a shrunk panel, and like
green timber, warp, warp.

    (i)   Who is the speaker? To whom does he speak?
    (ii)   Who is 'This fellow', and who is to be joined in marriage to
           the person addressed?
    (iii) Why has the person addressed chosen to be married in this
           way? Is the marriage expected to last for a long time?

D8 Why would you be so fond to overcome
The bonny prizer of the humorous duke?
Your praise is come too swiftly home before you.
Know you not, master, to some kind of men
Their graces serve them but as enemies?
No more do yours.

    (i)   Who is the speaker? Who is his 'master'?
    (ii)   What is the event he refers to? Who is 'the humorous duke'?
    (iii) Why does the speaker warn the person addressed? What
           does this person decide to do?

**E Critical
Appreciation**
In written examinations, these present passages from the play, with one
or two questions inviting your comments. You need not restrict yourself
entirely to the material before you, but extend your response to take in

other relevant issues or comparable situations in the rest of the play. Some examination boards allow candidates to take their copies of the play into the examination room, asking them to re-read the specified sections of the play.

E1   Read *Act 1*, Scene 1, lines 36–109 ('Know you where you are, sir?' . . . 'as they did in the golden world'). Discuss Shakespeare's art of exposition from your reading of the passage.

E2   Read *Act 1*, Scene 3, lines 1–81 ('Why, cousin; why, Rosalind' . . . 'I cannot live out of her company.'). Consider the dramatic effects of the changes from prose to verse when Rosalind is banished by her uncle.

E3   Read *Act 2*, Scene 4, lines 19–57 ('O Corin, that thou knew'st how I do love her.' . . . 'but it grows something stale with me.'). Compare the different expressions of love in the play and in this passage.

E4   After re-reading the passage from *Act 5*, Scene 4, lines 24–99 ('from hence I go To make these doubts all even.' . . . '*Still music. Enter* Hymen'), comment on Shakespeare's techniques of 'filling in' for the passage of time.

F   Essays   These will usually give you a specific topic to discuss, or perhaps a question that must be answered, in writing, *with a reasoned argument*. They *never* want you to tell the story of the play—so don't! Your examiner—or teacher—has read the play, and does not need to be reminded of it. Relevant quotations will always help you to make your points more strongly.

F1   Compare the relationship between Oliver and Orlando with that of Duke Senior and Duke Frederick.

F2   What impressions of life at the court do we gain from Charles and Le Beau?

F3   Show how Rosalind's wit and humour conceal an inner sadness.

F4   By comparing her behaviour towards Orlando at court and in the Forest, show what freedom Rosalind gained by changing her costume.

F5   Describe in detail your reaction to the character of Rosalind.

F6   Do you agree that Celia is completely over-shadowed by Rosalind? How would you describe the character of Celia?

F7 Show how several characters reveal their natures by their comments on Sir Roland de Boys.

F8 In *As You Like It*, nothing very much happens. What do you consider to be the most important way (or ways) in which Shakespeare compensates for this lack of action?

F9 'Their graces serve them but as enemies': discuss the themes of virtue, and the envy of virtue, in *As You Like It*.

F10 'Touchstone and Jaques are extraneous to the plot but essential to the play.' With reference to *either* Touchstone *or* Jaques, explain this statement. Do you agree with it?

F11 'Both Rosalind and Phoebe try to bring their lovers to a better understanding of love; their methods are the same, but the audience must react differently.' Why do you think this might have been said?

F12 'Duke Senior and his followers escape to the Forest of Arden; but this does not mean that they are escapists.' Can you explain this statement?

G Projects In some schools, students are asked to do more 'free-ranging' work, which takes them outside the text—but which should always be relevant to the play. Such Projects may demand skills other than reading and writing: design and artwork for instance, may be involved. Sometimes a 'portfolio' of work is assembled over a considerable period of time; and this can be presented to the examiner as part of the student's work for assessment.

The availability of resources will, obviously, do much to determine the nature of the Projects; but this is something that only the local teachers will understand. However, there is always help to be found in libraries, museums, and art galleries.

Suggestions **G1** The Good Life.

G2 The court fool.

G3 Great actresses in *As You Like It*.

G4 Rural Retreats.

G5 Pastoral Literature.

G6 Shakespeare's Globe Theatre

Background

England c. 1599

When Shakespeare was writing *As You Like It*, most people still believed that the sun went round the earth. They were taught that this was a divinely ordered scheme of things, and that—in England—God had instituted a Church and ordained a Monarchy for the right government of the land and the populace.

'The past is a foreign country; they do things differently there.'

L. P. Hartley

Government   For most of Shakespeare's life, the reigning monarch of England was Queen Elizabeth I. With her counsellors and ministers, she governed the nation (population about five million) from London, although not more than half a million people inhabited the capital city. In the rest of the country, law and order were maintained by the land-owners and enforced by their deputies. The average man had no vote—and his wife had no rights at all.

Religion   At this time, England was a Christian country. All children were baptized, soon after they were born, into the Church of England; they were taught the essentials of the Christian faith, and instructed in their duty to God and to humankind.

Marriages were performed, and funerals conducted, only by the licensed clergy and in accordance with the Church's rites and ceremonies. Attendance at divine service was compulsory, and absences (without good—medical—reason) could be punished by fines. By such means, the authorities were able to keep some check on the populace—recording births, marriages, and deaths; being alert to any religious nonconformity, which could be politically dangerous; and ensuring a minimum of orthodox instruction through the official 'Homilies' which were regularly preached from the pulpits of all parish churches throughout the realm.

Following Henry VIII's break away from the Church of Rome, all people in England were able to hear the church services *in their own language.* The Book of Common Prayer was used in every church, and an English translation of the Bible was read aloud in public. The Christian religion had never been so well taught before!

Education

School education reinforced the Church's teaching. From the age of four, boys might attend the 'petty school' (French '*petite école*') to learn the rudiments of reading and writing along with a few prayers; some schools also included work with numbers. At the age of seven, the boy was ready for the grammar school (if his father was willing and able to pay the fees).

Here, a thorough grounding in Latin grammar was followed by translation work and the study of Roman authors, paying attention as much to style as to matter. The arts of fine writing were thus inculcated from early youth.

A very few students proceeded to university; these were either clever scholarship boys, or else the sons of noblemen. Girls stayed at home, and acquired domestic and social skills—cooking, sewing, perhaps even music. The lucky ones might learn to read and write.

Language

At the start of the sixteenth century the English had a very poor opinion of their own language: there was little serious writing in English, and hardly any literature. Latin was the language of international scholarship, and Englishmen admired the eloquence of the Romans. They made many translations, and in this way they extended the resources of their own language, increasing its vocabulary and stretching its grammatical structures. French, Italian, and Spanish works were also translated and, for the first time, there were English versions of the Bible.

By the end of the century, English was a language to be proud of: it was rich in synonyms, capable of infinite variety and subtlety, and ready for all kinds of word-play—especially the *puns*, for which Shakespeare's English is renowned.

Drama

The great art-form of the Elizabethan and Jacobean age was its drama. The Elizabethans inherited a tradition of play-acting from the Middle Ages, and they reinforced this by reading and translating the Roman playwrights. At the beginning of the sixteenth century plays were performed by groups of actors, all-male companies (boys acted the female roles) who travelled from town to town, setting up their stages in open places (such as inn-yards) or, with the permission of the owner, in the hall of some noble house. The touring companies continued, in the provinces, into the seventeenth century; but in London, in 1576, a new building was erected for the performance of plays. This was the Theatre, the first purpose-built playhouse in England. Other playhouses followed, including Shakespeare's own theatre, the Globe, which was completed in 1599. The English drama reached new heights of eloquence.

There were those who disapproved, of course. The theatres, which brought large crowds together, could encourage the spread of disease—and dangerous ideas. During the summer, when the plague was at its worst, the playhouses were closed. A constant censorship was imposed, more or less severe at different times. The Puritan faction tried to close down the theatres, but—partly because there was royal favour for the drama, and partly because the buildings were outside the city limits—they did not succeed until 1642.

Theatre From contemporary comments and sketches—most particularly a drawing by a Dutch visitor, Johannes de Witt—it is possible to form some idea of the typical Elizabethan playhouse for which most of Shakespeare's plays were written. Hexagonal in shape, it had three roofed galleries encircling an open courtyard. The plain, high stage projected into the yard, where it was surrounded by the audience of standing 'groundlings'. At the back were two doors for the actors' entrances and exits, and between these doors was a curtained 'discovery space' (sometimes called an 'inner stage'). Above this was a balcony, used as a musicians' gallery or for the performance of scenes 'above', and projecting over part of the stage was a roof, supported on two pillars, which was painted with the sun, moon, and stars for the 'heavens'.

Underneath was space (concealed by curtaining) which could be used by characters ascending and descending through a trap-door in the stage. Costumes and properties were kept backstage in the 'tiring house'. The actors dressed lavishly, often wearing the secondhand clothes bestowed by rich patrons. Stage properties were important for defining a location, but the dramatist's own words were needed to explain the time of day, since all performances took place in the early afternoon.

A replica of Shakespeare's theatre, the Globe, has been built in London, and stands in Southwark, almost exactly on the Bankside site of the original.

Shakespeare's Globe, Southwark, London, England. Photograph by Richard Kalina.

William Shakespeare, 1564–1616

Elizabeth I was Queen of England when Shakespeare was born in 1564. He was the son of a tradesman who made and sold gloves in the small town of Stratford-upon-Avon, and he was educated at the grammar school in that town. Shakespeare did not go to university when he left school, but worked, perhaps, in his father's business. When he was eighteen he married Anne Hathaway, who became the mother of his daughter, Susanna, in 1583, and of twins in 1585.

There is nothing exciting, or even unusual, in this story; and from 1585 until 1592 there are no documents that can tell us anything at all about Shakespeare. But we have learned that in 1592 he was known in London, and that he had become both an actor and a playwright.

We do not know when Shakespeare wrote his first play, and indeed we are not sure of the order in which he wrote his works. If you look on page 130 at the list of his writings and their approximate dates, you will see how he started by writing plays on subjects taken from the history of England. No doubt this was partly because he was always an intensely patriotic man—but he was also a very shrewd business-man. He could see that the theatre audiences enjoyed being shown their own history, and it was certain that he would make a profit from this kind of drama.

The plays in the next group are mainly comedies, with romantic love stories of young people who fall in love with one another, and at the end of the play marry and live happily ever after.

At the end of the sixteenth century the happiness disappears, and Shakespeare's plays become melancholy, bitter, and tragic. This change may have been caused by some sadness in the writer's life (one of his twins died in 1596). Shakespeare, however, was not the only writer whose works at this time were very serious. The whole of England was facing a crisis. Queen Elizabeth I was growing old. She was greatly loved, and the people were sad to think she must soon die; they were also afraid, for the queen had never married, and so there was no child to succeed her.

When James I came to the throne in 1603, Shakespeare continued to write serious drama—the great tragedies and the plays based on Roman history (such as *Julius Caesar*) for which he is most famous. Finally, before he retired from the theatre, he wrote another set of comedies. These all have the same theme: they tell of happiness which is lost, and then found again.

Shakespeare returned from London to Stratford, his home town. He was rich and successful, and he owned one of the biggest houses in the town. He died in 1616.

Shakespeare also wrote two long poems, and a collection of sonnets. The sonnets describe two love-affairs, but we do not know who the lovers were. Although there are many public documents concerned with his career as a writer and a business-man, Shakespeare has hidden his personal life from us. A nineteenth-century poet, Matthew Arnold, addressed Shakespeare in a poem, and wrote 'We ask and ask—Thou smilest, and art still'.

Approximate Dates of Composition of Shakespeare's Works

Period	Comedies	History plays	Tragedies	Poems
I	Comedy of Errors Taming of the Shrew	Henry VI, part 1 Henry VI, part 2	Titus Andronicus	
1594	Two Gentlemen of Verona Love's Labour's Lost	Henry VI, part 3 Richard III King John		Venus and Adonis Rape of Lucrece
II	Midsummer Night's Dream Merchant of Venice	Richard II Henry IV, part 1	Romeo and Juliet	
1599	Merry Wives of Windsor Much Ado About Nothing As You Like It	Henry IV, part 2 Henry V		Sonnets
III	Twelfth Night Troilus and Cressida		Julius Caesar Hamlet Othello	
1608	Measure for Measure All's Well That Ends Well		Timon of Athens King Lear Macbeth Antony and Cleopatra Coriolanus	
IV	Pericles Cymbeline			
1613	The Winter's Tale The Tempest	Henry VIII		

Exploring As You Like It *in the Classroom*

Goodies, baddies, lovers, lords and shepherds bring the world of *As You Like It* to life, in scenes revealing the cutting sophistication of palace life as well as the mellow realities of rural retreats.

This section will suggest a range of approaches in the classroom, to help students access, enjoy and understand this romantic drama.

Ways into the Play

Students may feel an antipathy towards the study of Shakespeare. The imaginative and enthusiastic teacher, with the help of this edition of the play, will soon break this down!

Town or country

One of the main threads running through the play is the contrast between town and country life. Ask students to list what they see as the advantages and disadvantages of both modes of living. Where would their ideal home be? If possible, tell them Aesop's tale of The Town Mouse and the Country Mouse (e.g. from http://www.bartleby.com/17/1/7.html) and ask them to create a cartoon strip that relates the story.

Every picture tells a story

Ask your students to look at some pictures related to *As You Like It*; for example, paintings from the Shakespeare Illustrated site (see *Further Reading and Resources* on page 139) and make a guess as to the type of people depicted as well as the possible words and feelings behind the pictures. Later on, when they know more about the play you can ask them to hazard a guess as to the moment(s) depicted in the play.

Navigating the play

Your students may need some help and practice at finding their way around a Shakespeare play. After explaining the division into acts, scenes and lines, challenge them to look up some references – such as those below – as quickly as possible. Ask them to discuss the possible meaning of the lines and to use the lines to hazard a guess at some of the elements of the plot of the story.

Act 1, Scene 1, lines 96–97 *(Can you tell if Rosalind, the duke's daughter, be banished with her father?)*

Act 1, Scene 3, lines 101–2 *(Rosalind: Why, whither shall we go?*
Celia: To seek my uncle in the Forest of Arden.)

Act 2, Scene 7, lines 139–40 *(All the world's a stage / And all the men and women merely players.)*

Act 3, Scene 3, lines 239–40 *(Jaques: 'Rosalind' is your love's name?*
Orlando: Yes, just.)

Improvisation

Working on one of these improvisations may help students access some of the ideas behind the drama.

a) Ask students to work in pairs. They should take on the role of siblings who have been left at home alone. The older one has been left in charge, and is also responsible for all the money they have been given. S/he resents the younger sibling, and wants to make his/her life awkward. Ask them to improvise a conversation involving the younger one coming to ask for money for something important to him/her.

b) Ask students to work in small groups. They are on an adventure – entering a deep, dark forest. Through their words and actions, they must reveal both how they feel (e.g. excited, nervous, tired) and what they experience. The characters in their improvisation should react in different ways.

c) Students should work in small groups. They should create a scene for a soap opera (e.g. Hollyoaks, Eastenders) in which one of the characters (A) is in disguise. S/he hears another character professing their love for A. How does A react? They should aim for a humorous scene.

Setting the Scene

The Forest of Arden

Much of the action of the play takes place in a forest. Shakespeare uses the forest as a sort of rural retreat in which the characters can leave behind the usual constraints of their lives and discover themselves. Duke Senior and his followers live in the forest, as do various country folk. Ask students to give each other a 'guided tour' of the forest. Working in pairs, one should describe the forest to the other (who has closed eyes). The tour could be actually moving around if you have room, or with students seated. They should comment on what they can see, hear and feel in the environment before swapping over and continuing the guided tour as they move to another area of the forest.

Worlds apart

There are two main settings for the play:

- the palace: the supposedly civilised world of the nobility and their followers
- the Forest of Arden: most of the action takes place here in this rather idyllic and pastoral setting.

Challenge students to create a 'mood board' for each setting, where they gather images, words, colours, etc. that reflect the contrast of the two different settings. These can be used for designing a set for the play.

Verses of love

If possible arrange some cross-curricular collaboration to bring the songs and verses of the play to life. Ask music department colleagues or students to work out the melody of 'It was a lover and his lass' (a score is provided on page 109). Then ask students to work out suitable music for other verses in the play, e.g. Amiens' song (Act 2, Scene 5, lines 1–8) or Orlando's verse (Act 3, Scene 3, lines 72–78).

Keeping Track of the Action

It's important to give students opportunities to 'digest' and reflect upon their reading, so that they may take ownership of the play.

Reading journal

As you read through the play, help students to trace and understand the story by asking them to keep a journal in which they record what happens. They can also record their reactions and thoughts about the action and the characters. Their responses can remain focused through specific questions (from the teacher) to answer.

Actor's blog

Ask each student to imagine they are an actor playing one of the main characters in the play. As you read, perform or watch the play, they must pay particular attention to their character, and write an online journal or blog on their character. The blog can record such things as:

- what they are trying to achieve with their character
- enjoyable parts of the action
- difficult parts to act
- how their character is developing
- what they think of their character
- how their character feels.

If you can set up a proper blog for them, then other students/characters will be able to post their comments on the actor's blog.

Some theatre websites have comments/audio from the actors about their parts that can provide a model for their reflections.

The Arden Bugle

Ask students to write news reports for the local newspaper, reflecting the action in the play. Possible news reports and features include:

- the death of Sir Roland de Boys (before the play begins)
- the wrestling match
- the banishment of Rosalind
- Duke Senior's life in the forest
- Orlando saving his brother from a lion
- a marriage boom
- my life as a man: Rosalind.

Changing fortunes

The play begins with Orlando and finishes with Rosalind. In between, their lives are transformed. Encourage students to chart the fortunes of Rosalind and Orlando by means of drawing a graph for each character, with a scale of 0–10 on one axis to represent their fortunes, and the relevant scenes labelled on the other axis. The fortune graphs should reflect how well each character is going throughout the play.

Characters

Students of all ages need to come to an understanding of the characters: their motivations, their relationships and their development.

Rosalind

Rosalind is a complex character. She is bright, witty, kind, independent and clever. She successfully disguises herself as Ganymede, fooling other characters, notably Orlando and Phoebe. The success of the play depends on the appropriate casting of Rosalind. Ask students to act as a casting director, casting her part for a new film or stage version of the play. First, they must create a character profile for Rosalind, containing information about them (known and surmised). Next, they must decide on which actress they would like to take the part and explain why. Finally, they should give the actress important information about the character, and information about how to play the part.

A melancholy character

Jaques is a complete contrast to the buoyant and lively character of Rosalind. He is a melancholy follower of Duke Senior. In Act 2, Scene 7 he ponders on his desire for a fool's clothing ('motley coat' Act 2, Scene 7, line 43). Ask students to design a costume for Jaques that will reflect his downhearted approach to life.

A different perspective

Allowing your students the opportunity to think, write and talk as one of the characters, gives them a new and illuminating perspective on the character(s). Here are some possible tasks:

a) Act 1, Scene 3: Celia keeps a video diary, in which she reveals how she feels about her father and her father's actions in banishing Rosalind.

b) Act 2, Scene 2: Duke Frederick is interviewed about the disappearance of his daughter.

c) Act 2, Scene 4 & Act 3, Scene 3: Touchstone confides in his diary about how he feels about life in the forest.

d) Act 3, Scene 6 & Act 5, Scene 4: A newspaper report reveals how Phoebe feels about being tricked into marriage.

e) Epilogue: Rosalind writes her own verse summing up the action in the play.

Themes

Film poster

Once you have explored some of the themes of the play, ask students to create a film poster which gives a flavour of some of the main themes. As a model, show them a previous film poster (e.g. http://www.imdb.com/title/tt0450972/mediaindex) and ask them to analyse how the poster works, before creating their own.

Love: pleasure or pain?

This is a play about love, but love can be the cause of both delight and suffering. Ask students to find examples of how love is portrayed in the play, as well as exploring:

- which characters suffer due to love
- who shows the deepest and most sincere love
- whose love is most/least convincing
- whether love is a positive emotion, overall.

Ask volunteers to take on some of the roles (e.g. Rosalind, Orlando, Silvius, Phoebe) then 'hotseat' them, asking them about their views on love.

Gender investigation

Rosalind's decision to dress as a man enables her to act and talk differently to when she is dressed as a woman. The audience in Shakespeare's day would have enjoyed the layered irony that the character of Rosalind would have been played by a boy anyway. Use the play to encourage students to consider how male and female roles have changed over time. In Shakespeare's time there were fixed ideas about how men and women should act. Ask them to consider:

- why Rosalind and Celia go to find Rosalind's father
- why Rosalind dresses as a man
- why they take Touchstone with them
- whether dressing as a man changes Rosalind in any way.

Ask them to consider whether we still have fixed ideas of how men and women should behave.

Envy

Envy is one of the seven deadly sins (the others being lust, gluttony, greed, sloth, wrath and pride). Ask students to write a definition of what they think envy means, before comparing their definition with a dictionary definition. Discuss why envy is seen as a sin, what it does to people and who displays it in the play.

Shakespeare's Language

Prose and verse

Shakespeare uses prose and verse for different reasons. Traditionally, prose was put in the mouths of comics or ordinary characters, while verse was spoken by nobility and lovers. In this play it is generally the topic that dictates the form. Ask students to investigate when and why verse and prose are used by the same characters, e.g.

- Orlando, talking to Adam (Act 1, Scene 1) then to Rosalind (Act 1, Scene 2)
- Oliver, talking to Charles (Act 1, Scene 1) and to Rosalind and Celia (Act 4, Scene 3).

Soliloquy

Perhaps Shakespeare's best known soliloquy is Jaques' 'All the world's a stage…' speech (Act 2, Scene 7, lines 139–166). Challenge students to learn the whole of this famous speech. Ask them to look at how simile and metaphor are used in this extended metaphor, by highlighting the examples they find. Being from Jaques, it is no surprise that there is an overall negative tone to the soliloquy, so ask them to change the tone of the speech, focusing on changing the images into positive ones.

Songs

As well as the verse and prose, the play contains a number of songs. The songs are generally in keeping with the light-hearted nature of love that runs through the play. Ask students to study the form of one of the songs (e.g. the regular rhythm and rhyme) and ask them to imitate this form by creating a song about one of the characters in the play.

Exploring with Drama

Book the hall or push back the desks, because the best way to study a great play is through drama. Students of all ages will benefit from a dramatic encounter with *As You Like It*. They will enjoy the opportunity to act out a scene or two, or to explore the situations through improvisation; for example, putting a character in the 'hot seat' for questioning by others.

Tableaux

Ask your students, in groups, to create a tableau which contains all the main characters from the play. The positions of the characters should say something about their relationships and position within the play. The students could bring the tableaux to life briefly, by each saying something in character.

Rolling theatre

Focusing on the 'All the world's a stage' soliloquy (Act 2, Scene 7, lines 139–166), divide students into groups and ask each group to take on one of the seven acts or ages of man. Each group should put together an improvisation to act out their particular age. Once the improvisations have been practised, ask each group to perform their age in order, one after the other, so that all the scenes blend to form a performance of each of the seven ages of man.

A reduced version

Test their understanding of the plot by asking groups to create a reduced version of the whole play. They will first need to decide on the key events and the essential characters, and they should try to include some quotations in their version.

Romantic comedy

There are a number of scenes which provide warm and gentle comedy for the audience. Let students enjoy acting out one of these scenes, e.g.

- Act 3, Scene 6 (Silvius, Phoebe and Rosalind)
- Act 4, Scene 1 (Rosalind and Orlando)
- Act 5, Scene 1 (Touchstone and Audrey)

Select an appropriate extract and put the students into small groups, appointing one as a director. The director must then direct the other student(s) to give an action reading of the scene; they can use their scripts but must act out the lines. Encourage them to use timing, actions, voices and expressions to bring out the comedy of the scene.

Writing about *As You Like It*

If your students have to write about *As You Like It* for coursework or for examinations, you may wish to give them this general guidance:

- Read the question or task carefully, highlight the key words and answer all parts of the question.
- Planning is essential. Plan what will be in each paragraph. You can change your plan if necessary.
- Avoid retelling the story.
- *As You Like It* is a play – so consider the impact or effect on the audience.
- Use the Point, Evidence, Explanation (PEE) structure to explain points.
- Adding Evaluation (PEEE!) will gain you higher marks.
- Keep quotations short.
- Avoid referring to a film version of the play, unless this is part of your task.

Further Reading and Resources

General

Bryson, Bill, *Shakespeare* (Harper Perennial, 2008).

Fantasia, Louis, *Instant Shakespeare: A Practical Guide for Actors, Directors and Teachers* (A & C Black, 2002).

Greer, Germaine, *Shakespeare: A Very Short Introduction* (Oxford, 2002).

Hall, Peter, *Shakespeare's Advice to the Players* (Oberon Books, 2003).

Holden, Anthony, *Shakespeare: His Life and Work* (Abacus, 2002).

Kneen, Judith, *Teaching Shakespeare from Transition to Test* (Oxford University Press, 2004).

McConnell, Louise, *Exit, Pursued By A Bear – Shakespeare's Characters, Plays, Poems, History and Stagecraft* (Bloomsbury, 2003).

McLeish, Kenneth and Unwin, Stephen, *A Pocket Guide to Shakespeare's Plays* (Faber and Faber, 1998).

Muirden, James, *Shakespeare in a Nutshell: A Rhyming Guide to All the Plays* (Constable 2004).

Wood, Michael, *In Search of Shakespeare* (BBC, 2003).

Children's/Students' Books

Carpenter, Humphrey, *More Shakespeare Without the Boring Bits* (Viking, 1997).

Richard Cuddington, *Easy Reading Shakespeare: The Bard in Bite-Size Verse Volume 2* (Book Guild Ltd, 2006).

Ganeri, Anita, *What They Don't Tell You About Shakespeare* (Hodder, 1996).

Garfield, Leon, *Shakespeare Stories II* (Puffin 1997).

Garfield, Leon (Ed), *As You Like It (The Animated Tales)* (Methuen 1994).

Lamb, Charles and Mary, *Tales from Shakespeare* (Puffin edition 1987).

McCaughrean, Geraldine, *Stories from Shakespeare* (Orion, 1997).

Williams, Marcia, *Bravo, Mr William Shakespeare!* (Walker, 2001).

Websites

The Complete Works of William Shakespeare
http://the-tech.mit.edu/Shakespeare/

Elizabethan pronunciation
Including information on insults.
http://www.renfaire.com/Language/index.html

Encyclopaedia Britannica's Guide to Shakespeare
http://search.eb.com/shakespeare

HBO Films – website for the 2006 film of As You Like It
http://www.hbo.com/films/asyoulikeit

The Royal Shakespeare Company website
As well as information on the theatre company, there are resources
on the plays and the life and times of Shakespeare.
http://www.rsc.org.uk

The Shakespeare Birthplace Trust
Information on his works, life and times.
http://www.shakespeare.org.uk/homepage

Shakespeare's Globe
Information on The Globe Theatre, London.
http://www.shakespeares-globe.org

Shakespeare Illustrated
An excellent source of paintings and pictures based on
Shakespeare's plays.
http://shakespeare.emory.edu/illustrated_index.cfm

Spark Notes: As You Like It
An online study guide.
http://www.sparknotes.com/shakespeare/asyoulikeit

Mr William Shakespeare and the Internet
A comprehensive guide to Shakespeare resources on the internet.
http://shakespeare.palomar.edu

Film, video, DVD, and audio

As You Like It, featuring Laurence Olivier (1936) DVD
As You Like It, BBC Shakespeare DVD
As You Like It, featuring James Fox (1992) DVD
As You Like It, Directed by Kenneth Brannagh (2006) DVD
Shakespeare: The Animated Tales (1992) DVD
As You Like It, BBC Audiobooks (2006)